A REPORT ON THE AMERICAN JESUITS

A REPORT ON THE

American Jesuits

Text by JOHN LaFARGE, S.J.

Photographs by MARGARET BOURKE-WHITE

NEW YORK

Farrar, Straus and Cudahy

Imprimi potest

Thomas E. Henneberry, S.J.
Provincial: New York Province

Nihil obstat

John M. A. Fearns, S.T.D.
Censor Librorum

Imprimatur

✠ Francis Cardinal Spellman
Archbishop of New York

All photographs in this volume
by permission of *Life* Magazine

CONTENTS

PART ONE

BACKGROUND

FOLLOWERS OF ST. IGNATIUS OF LOYOLA

FRIEND OF THE YOUNG: The late Rev. Daniel A. Lord, S. J., playwright and prolific author.

SEISMOLOGIST AND GEOLOGIST: Rev. Daniel Linehan, S.J. at work on the Kennebec River, Maine.

WATERFRONT PRIEST: Rev. Dennis J. Comey, S. J. and pier officials at Philadelphia docks.

FOREIGN SERVICE SCHOOL: Rev. Frank L. Fadner,
S.J. at the Electronic Language Laboratory of the
Georgetown School of Foreign Service, working
with techniques adapted by U.N. translators.

HONDURAS MISSIONARY: Rev. Gregory B. Sontag, S. J. reading his Office on the porch of Middlebank Church, British Honduras.

In the "Father's Hut": Rev. Urban Kramer, S. J. tells stories to children of Rancho Dolores, British Honduras.

THEOLOGIAN: Rev. John Courtney Murray, S. J. editor of *Theological Studies,* Woodstock College, Maryland.

AVIATOR: Rev. John J. Higgins, S. J., chief flying instructor at Parks College of Aeronautical Technology, St. Louis University.

FISHERMAN: Rev. John P. Sullivan, S.J. fishing off San Pedro Cay, in the white cassock worn by missionaries in tropical areas.

ON MISSION ROUNDS: Rev. John T. Newell, S.J. pauses to read his Office on journey to remote mountain village in Republic of Honduras.

OLDEST JESUIT: Rev. Laurence J. Kenny, S. J., who was 91 on Columbus Day, 1955, has served longer in the classroom than any other American Jesuit.

ORIGINS

WHO are the men whom you see depicted in these pages? Perhaps a little explanation would be helpful. Some years ago, after the author had joined the Jesuits, a devout old Protestant neighbor in my hometown was much interested in the mysterious step that I had taken. "Tell me," Miss Bessie asked of my sister, "just what has happened to your brother?" "He is now," said my sister, choosing accurate language, "a member of the Society of Jesus." Raising her eyes devoutly to heaven, Miss Bessie murmured: "So, I trust, are all of us."

Miss Bessie was not entirely mistaken. True Christians are followers of Jesus of Nazareth, the Founder of Christianity, and it is the ideal of all of us to be members of that *ekklesia* or congregation or church that He established in order to carry His sacred doctrine and His life-giving presence to all men and all places until the end of time. All Christians, as is obvious, are bound by what He has commanded: His precepts of justice, purity, fraternal love. But some wish to go further. Jesus was not satisfied with laying down rules of living for all men. He invited some people, among His closest followers, to practice special counsels. They are invited to abandon their earthly possessions, and to live in poverty and toil. Like Him, they would forego the joys of the married state and lead a life of perpetual chastity. They would practice in their own lives that virtue of religious obedience which He observed at every moment toward His heavenly Father. They would dedicate themselves, in other words, to the observance of the Counsels as well as of the Commandments, and they would do this not only in an individual capacity, but in communities or religious Orders.

This is obviously a broad program, which leaves a vast scope of difference as to the many different *ways* or spiritual techniques by which men and women may interpret this higher following of the Saviour. Hence the great variety of religious communities within the Catholic church, whose history has been marked by three great waves of religious Orders. The first of these, the monks, associated their religious life with the cultivation of the soil and a communal tenure of a particular landed property. They were, in the picturesque phrase, "serfs

of the Lord," *ascripti glebae,* vowed to stability upon a particular territory. Detached from the ordinary life of men, they devoted themselves to contemplation, humble labor along with
long-term, patient scholastic pursuits and solemn liturgical
observance. Such particularly are the older Orders of the
Church, as the Benedictines, Cistercians, and Carthusians.

In the second great wave, accompanying the flowering of
medieval culture, came the marvelous development of the
Friars, of a much more mobile type, more engaged in outward
activities for the neighbor's salvation. Such are the three great
branches of the Franciscan Order, the Friars Preachers—Black-
friars or Dominicans, and the Carmelites or White Friars. The
close of the Middle Ages, the dawn of the modern era, was
marked by a third development, that of the Clerks Regular,
who were still more free of certain monastic observances, with
a corresponding stress upon mobility and adaptability to apostolic ends. Despite the great differences in the observances of
these various types of religious communities and their differ-
ing costumes, liturgical or community practices, manner of
studies, and other variations, certain principles are common to
all, and the variations are far less important than the agree-
ment.

The Jesuits, accordingly, are comparative newcomers in this
series, since they began in the first half of the sixteenth century. Their founder, Ignatius of Loyola, was a Spanish knight
who underwent a profound religious experience and called
the little group of university men whom he gathered around
him the Company (*Compañía*) of Jesus—a Spanish military
term which was rendered *Society* in Latin and other languages,

such as English. (The French still refer to the Jesuits as *La Compagnie de Jésus.*) Ignatius and his little band dedicated themselves to limitless work for the spiritual salvation of their neighbors, in any part of the world and in any circumstance.

Their mode of life and their plan of action were to be modeled upon the life led by the personal followers of Jesus of Nazareth, or rather upon the example of the Saviour as set in His own historical life and described in the Gospels. In every way feasible they strove to make His attitude and His sentiments their own—toward individuals and toward the world—in a very special and intimate sense. Outwardly they would live, as Ignatius prescribed in the Constitutions that he drew up for his Order, in much the same way as any abstemious and poor priest in the ranks of the Church. In this way they differed from the older religious Orders, which required a certain fixed costume or "habit," practised the chanting or recitation in common of the Divine Office—the Church's daily official vocal prayer, and observed a number of obligatory austerities over and above those prescribed for all Catholics by the Church. Compensating for this lack of certain outward observances, the members of the Society pledged themselves to a specially exacting fulfillment of the vow of obedience to superiors in the Order, and through them to the Church and to God Himself. They likewise bound themselves by a special vow of obedience to the Pope, as the visible head of Christ's Church on earth.

How did they begin?

In the year 1528 a thirty-seven-year-old Spanish nobleman, Iñigo de Loyola, came to be enrolled at the University of Paris.

Seven years before, in the service of the King of Spain, he had been wounded in a battle at Pamplona. During his long convalescence in his native castle high in the Basque Pyrenees, he had experienced a deep change of heart and conceived an immense desire to follow in the footsteps of such great saints of the Church as Augustine, Dominic, and Francis, and to devote himself chivalrously to the service of Our Lord and Master Jesus Christ. He began, accordingly, a life of pilgrimage and penance, eventually changing his native name Iñigo to the Latin, Ignatius, in honor of the great martyr, St. Ignatius of Antioch.

During a time of retirement, penance, and intensive prayer in a cave near the village of Manresa, Ignatius received a profound revelation of the steps to be followed by one who seriously wishes to reform his life and offer himself wholeheartedly to God's service. The results of this experience he summarized in a compact booklet, rather like a notebook in character, under the title *The Spiritual Exercises.*

The aim of this book, or rather of the *Exercises* themselves, was to enable a person to use with God's help the powers of his own soul, in order to reach a permanent decision as to the type of life God would wish him to embrace, and the means he should adopt in order to follow it. The decision was to be reached not according to some abstract theory but by the light of the teachings of Jesus Christ as given to us by His Church and of His own personal example as seen in the Gospels. Perhaps we could sum it up by saying that the *Exercises* are a decisive, dynamic reflection on the Gospels.

To an extent and fullness that perhaps had never been

accomplished before, Ignatius celebrated the greatness of God
and the greatness of human freedom. The directions and counsels of St. Ignatius for the time of the *Exercises* and for the life
to be built upon them are not magical conjurations, nor me-
thodical schemes of prayer and work which would compel God
to act; they are signs that a free creature is ready to heed the
call of the Supreme Lord, relying upon His grace. They hold
one in a certain uncertainty. God determines the way and the
manner that calls each person to his special and irreplaceable
task in the whole. This teaching is far removed from the activ-
ism of a Pelagius who held that man could work out his
salvation without grace, and also from a sort of passivity im-
plying the utter uselessness of all natural human powers.

What Ignatius had learned for himself he had learned for
others. Coming to Paris to prepare himself for the priesthood, his first thought was to communicate the treasures of the
Spiritual Exercises to a few chosen friends who would grasp
them, reform their lives accordingly, and thereby prepare
themselves to go forth and set the world on fire for Christ.
They were of different nationalities: a Portuguese, four
Spaniards (of whom one, Francis Xavier, was a fellow Basque),
and a Savoyard, Peter Faber (Pierre Lefèvre), who alone was
already ordained a priest. Shortly afterward several others decided to join the little Company, and they first formed the
idea of making their way to Jerusalem in order to evangelize
the Holy Land. They pledged themselves to the service of God
at the Parisian shrine of Montmartre in 1534. Three years
afterward Pope Paul III permitted the rest to be ordained
priests. On September 27, 1540, the Pope issued a solemn con-

firmation of the Order (*Regimini Militantis Ecclesiae*), and
the Company pronounced solemn vows in Rome at St. Paul's
Outside-the-Walls. In 1544 Pope Paul III removed his previ-
ous restrictions as to the number to be admitted to the Order,
and in 1550 approved a second formula of its Rule or Institute. In 1546 the same Pope allowed Ignatius to admit a certain number of "spiritual coadjutors," priests who would assist
the work of its solemnly professed members. Later on, a similar provision was made for members who would not become
priests, and were known—as they still are—as "coadjutor
brothers."

Ignatius, after long and anxious deliberation, accepted in
1541 his colleagues' choice of him as their first Superior
General, which position he held until his death on July 31,
1556. Soon the great outlines of the Order appeared. Ignatius
worked for several years (1547–50) upon its Constitutions. It
was not until 1558 that the Order's first general congregation
adopted the Constitutions as a whole. The Constitutions con-
sist of an Examen (published first about 1546), then the Constitutions proper, which are in ten parts. The Examen is a
sort of questionnaire for candidates, written so that those who
wish to join the Order will obtain certainty as to what is
expected of them, and the Order itself will know what to think
of the person who applied.

The Constitutions are the most comprehensive rule of any
Order, yet the basic idea is rather simple. They express the
concept of the *Exercises* themselves: God is the End of creation
and redemption; all else is only a means to that End which
men have the power to accept or reject, with a corresponding

moral responsibility. Man must realize this distinction, and carry it out generously in practice. The service of God is the praise of His infinite majesty, goodness, and wisdom. In his Constitutions Ignatius uses 140 times the expression "the service of God." But God is served through the following of Christ in the service of the Church: the living, teaching, suffering, redeeming and sanctifying Christ.

To achieve this great end, Ignatius stresses three fundamental means. The first of these is the life of prayer, without which everyone else would be arid and meaningless: prayer—individual, personal prayer with the Father alone in one's room and in the secret of one's heart, as well as participation in the sacramental and liturgical life of the Church. Prayer for him is very closely associated with the work of an active apostolate and its demands on time and energy; hence there is not the stress on official and lengthy prayer that you find in the old monastic Orders. In short, obedience and love, practiced in a thoroughly prayerful spirit, are as important in the spiritual life of the individual as any formal practice of prayer. Yet Ignatius went out of his way to commend the practice of long prayers and devotion to the sacred liturgy, which he himself keenly relished. Today, in nearly every country, Jesuits are in the forefront of a world-wide liturgical revival. In the United States, Father Gerald Ellard, S.J., of St. Mary's College, Kansas, is a veteran pioneer in the field of liturgical studies.

In the second place the Constitutions insist that the members must overcome selfishness, the corrupt element in our nature, so that the Holy Spirit can make us into new men formed in the image of Christ. This means a continual battle against selfishness, concupiscence, and cowardice. Over and over they stress the purification and the "perfecting of the instrument"—that is to say, the human agent of God's plans—through self-conquest, through suffering and self-denial. The climax of this expression is found in the famous eleventh rule of the Constitutions' Summary, where the members are exhorted to welcome a share in the sufferings of the Saviour and rejoice in companionship with Him in His "vesture" of trial and humiliation. But all this can be accomplished only by the grace of God, and man has no power except in so far as it is given him from on high.

The third element was distinctly Ignatian, namely, a highly comprehensive plan to enlist all natural circumstances and resources of the intellect and will and of the visible tangible world around us into the service of the Saviour. His scope excluded nothing that was good, that was holy, that could in any way further Christ's service. No sacrifice and no effort were to be too great. He emphasizes the need of generosity, broadness of scope, spontaneity of effort, readiness to dare, to conceive high ideals, to launch out into the depths. Yet he balances this holy extremism by an insistence on wisely giving preference to the works that are most important, permanent, comprehensive, and fundamental. Special talents are to be cultivated, yet always with an understanding of the whole.

Historically there was a certain peculiar opportuneness about this aspect of the Constitutions, as Father Becher* points out. They were formulated right after the Renaissance,

* Hubert Becher, S.J., *Die Jesuiten* (Munich, 1951).

23

in a period of exploration, adventure, and curiosity. So Ignatius projected a broad plan, and renounced for his followers some of the time-honored practices of the religious life toward which he was personally deeply sympathetic.

Yet this whole project would fall apart if not held together by some centralizing, cohesive element. So, as a counterweight, the Constitutions stress obedience. The idea of obedience itself was nothing new, even in the vigorous form in which Ignatius puts it. He used no expression stronger than those already employed by the great religious Founders—the Fathers of the Desert, Bernard, Benedict, Bruno, Dominic, Francis, and others. What was new was the departure from the chapter or capitular system in the government of the Order, with the corresponding prescription that this obedience was to be rendered to a General elected for life. The General Congregation, of delegates selected by the professed members, would function only for the selection of the General and for widely generalized legislation. The General appoints all superiors. He is accessible to all members through correspondence. At the same time he is pledged in obedience to the Pope as Vicar of Christ on earth. New also was the introduction of simple, perpetual vows—until then unheard of, but today an almost universal practice.

Striking, too, was the strict account of conscience, the manifestation which the member of the Order makes to his superior. In the Society it is the relationship of a son to a father, a relationship based upon a free choice and a mutual cooperation between superior and subject in their common work of following the Saviour.

Distinctive, too, in the Constitutions were the various grades of the priesthood and the brothers into which the Society was divided. The Jesuit was to see Christ in the superior: the outer rind of obedience was renunciation of one's self-will, but its inner core or sense was the following of Christ, the imitation of His own obedience to His heavenly Father.

It is easy to exaggerate the military character of the Society. True, Ignatius used certain military expressions—for he was himself a soldier—in terms taken from the military life of that time and from chivalry; nevertheless he prescribed no uniform. The dynamism of his little Company was not that of a military goose step marching blindly ahead, but was Christ's love for men even unto suffering on the Cross. It was not a Crimean Light Brigade hurling itself into the jaws of destruction, but a band of disciples practising reverence and love for God through and in His Son. This devoted service was to be coupled with a deep sense of fraternity and affection for one another and for all mankind.

Ignatius was profoundly grieved by the condition of the Church and the Hierarchy in his time. There were two ways he could attack the problem. One way was to retreat, as many good and pious men did at that time, into the inner world to forget as far as possible all that was happening around them, to lead a devout, recollected life and do one's business solely with God their Creator. At least that way, it was hoped, one might save one's own soul and commune with God even if others were descending on the road to hell.

The other course was the exact opposite, that of the radical reformer: to blast the Hierarchy of the Church, publicly to condemn corrupt bishops and the avaricious, disordered state of the Church in Rome. The reformer would attack the Church's sacramental system, the very, nature of its organization through the episcopate, the spiritual authority of its hierarchy, and would substitute private judgment; or even if there were no such radical, theological change, at least to express by violent denunciations one's grief over the disordered state of head and members.

Ignatius adopted neither course. He chose neither a retreat into the inner life nor a radical, outward, rhetorical reform but embarked on a third path, which was to find a remedy for the situation in the Church by discovering and practising the true spirit of the Church itself. He was firmly convinced that this true spirit, the genuine spirit or attitude of the Church, was the same as the spirit of Jesus Christ, because the same Holy Spirit, to use his words, governed the Church that spoke in the words of Christ Himself. It was Ignatius' genius, in the words of Henri de Lubac, or rather the effect of divine grace, that "at the threshold of the modern period he powerfully reaffirmed this bond of the Church and the Spirit. . . . It is thus he escaped the snare of pure interiority and became a giant in the line of men of the Church. And it was because of his correct intelligence of the mystery of the Church drawn from the mystic graces he received in prayer that he became one of the great spiritual teachers of all times."

Ignatius, therefore, sought to find the remedy for the Church by returning to the Founder, learning to live as He lived and to see all things from His viewpoint. The *Exercises* were not a disciplinary training ground for the service of the

Church, but a school for that Christlike manner of life which would make a man a worthy servant of the Church. Ignatius says that a man can find God in his life. He is to find out certain truths for himself, from his own deliberations, reaching his own decisions, using his own intelligence. No one makes the *Exercises* except from free choice. If they were to be imposed on anybody they would not be truly spiritual exercises. They are infinitely adaptable to circumstances and temperaments: to men and women, clergy and laity, to learned and ignorant, to young and old, as long as a few simple conditions are observed, such as a certain degree of recollection and removal from the busy affairs of life. They demand a quiet time, to use a modern phrase; a generous, sincere spirit and a humble dialogue with God Himself, keeping the soul open to God's suggestion and God's graces.

The power of any great idea results usually from the union of two opposites fused into one living dynamism. Such is the case of the spirit of the Society of Jesus as conceived by Ignatius. On the one hand he taught, following the example of his Divine Teacher Jesus Christ, an unlimited generosity, a perpetual "more"—always striving for, as he said, the more universal good; never content, always seeking the "greater glory of God." Yet, on the other hand, this striving for the illimitable was strictly governed by a vigorous virtue of prudence: a shrewd, careful, appreciation of what could and what could not be done. Limitless zeal was hedged about by holy obedience. All through the history of the Society we see the counterbalancing of two tendencies or influences: a passionate desire for greater and greater service on the one hand and, on the other, the exercise of prudence, discretion, careful appraisal of what is and is not possible. It is that union which gave such tremendous force to the idea of Christianity itself, which was to join, in the words of its Founder, the simplicity of the dove with the prudence of the serpent. It was no mere sacred enthusiasm lashing out in all directions without restraint, nor on the other was it just a carefully chiseled system of moralizing and meditation.

One of the most distinguishing features of Jesuit piety is that of the so-called examination of conscience which Ignatius recommended to all Christians and embodied as a principal feature in his own rule of life, an exercise to be performed for fifteen minutes twice every day. This examen is a continual return to the presence of the Creator and a reminder of our dependence on Him. At the same time it is a careful safeguard against the particular weaknesses that inhere in each individual by keeping check on one's own peculiarities.

Ignatius' little Company spread rapidly, especially in university towns like Bologna, Padua, Cologne, Louvain, Paris, and Coimbra. At the very beginning, so many wished to join the newly formed Society that its membership soon rose to over 200. At the death of Ignatius in 1556, there were already twelve provinces, of which three (India, Brazil, and Ethiopia, the last mentioned discontinued) were outside Europe. By 1563 there were 3,500 Jesuits in 130 houses and eighteen provinces; at the same time, the Jesuits solidified their status within the Church.

The innovations as to the structure of a religious Order

EXAMINATION OF CONSCIENCE

which Ignatius had intruded into his own Society were exposed for a while to a very real possibility of alteration through the higher authority of the Holy See. Pope St. Pius V (1556–62), a devoted friend and generous patron of the Society, was not without a feeling that the Society should confirm more to the example of the older Orders. He prescribed therefore certain restrictions which were later removed by Pope Gregory XIII (1572–85), who issued two solemn confirmations of the Society's Institute and established definitely that scholastics (candidates studying for the priesthood) and coadjutor brothers who had pronounced their simple perpetual vows at the conclusion of their noviceship were truly members of a religious Order, and that solemn vows, such as those which they uttered later in the course of their religious career were not required as a prerequisite for ordination to the priesthood.

Restrictions, likewise, that had been placed upon the Society by Pope Sixtus V (1589–90) were lifted by his second successor, Pope Gregory XIV ((1590–91).

The little Company lost no time in embarking upon its program of world-wide campaign for souls. In 1541 Francis Xavier, who died on the island of Sancian, near Canton, in 1552, sailed with three companions from Lisbon for the Indies. In 1549 five Jesuits went to Brazil, the first Jesuits in the Western Hemisphere. Year after years added to the far-flung role of the Society's missions: England (where Bl. Edmund Campion and his companions were martyred in 1581), Florida, Mexico, and Peru even before the end of the sixteenth century, as well as Ethiopia, the Congo, Japan, Angola, and Guinea; a little later, Canada, Chile, Paraguay, the Philippine

Islands, the Maronite Union in Syria, and China. Members of the Society—priests, scholastics, and coadjutor brothers—who had laid down their lives for the teaching and defense of the Christian faith, or who had shown the example of heroic faith, hope, charity, and wisdom in their lives, were honored by the Church with the title of Blessed, or even declared Saints by the elaborate process of canonization.

The Society's founder, Ignatius, and its greatest pioneer missionary, Francis Xavier, were canonized in 1622, and in gratitude all Jesuit priests say a special Mass of thanksgiving on March 12 of each year. Also raised to the high dignity of declared sainthood were three of the Society's youthful members—the novice Stanislaus Kostka, a Pole; Aloysius (Luigi) Gonzaga, an Italian, and John Berchmans, a Belgian. Later years brought the recognition of sainthood, some quite in our own time, to other spiritual heroes like Peter Claver (died, 1654), fiery Catalonian and apostle of Negro slaves in the New World; Alphonsus Rodriguez, Brother Porter of the Jesuit College of Majorca; the home missionaries John Francis Regis and Francis di Geronimo; the martyrs of Japan; Isaac Jogues and John de Brébeuf and their companions, the martyrs of Canada and New York; the catechist and apostle of Germany, Peter Canisius; the voluminous seventeenth-century writer and controversialist Robert Bellarmine; besides a host of the Blessed of practically every nationality, east and west. Last of all to be raised to the honors of the altar was that wholly unique figure, Joseph Pignatelli, who formed a link between the Society after its suppression in 1773 and its entire restoration in 1814.

In Dostoevski's *The Brothers Karamazov* the populace were bitterly disappointed after the death of the saintly elder or *starets,* Father Zossima, because his body began to decay. If he were a real saint, they reasoned, his body would remain incorrupt and so they could start pilgrimages to it. So Father Zossima, after all his good works, had failed in this final "test," even though Zossima himself during his lifetime had preached a much more solid form of Christian piety. If a Jesuit's body happened to stay incorrupt after his demise, as it did happen in the case of St. Francis Xavier and in other instances, well and good. However, the prize that Jesuits set upon these official Church declarations has a very different source—namely, that the declaration of sainthood or beatitude sets a seal of approval upon a man's *life* as such. It was particularly significant in the case of a scholastic like John Berchmans, or a coadjutor brother like Alphonsus Rodriguez, because it was a clear indication that a man could achieve, and had *de facto* achieved, the highest degree of Christian perfection by simply carrying out with complete fidelity the teachings and the ordinary manner of life of the Society—something that Ignatius found a little difficult to prove to some of his highly austere and mystical early companions. The saints, whoever they may be—and their number, living and dead, is beyond all counting in the Church—are simply the brothers and sisters whose lives are a pledge of our own hopes. They proclaim to us the wonders of that divine grace which, in one form or another, is at the call of all human beings, even the most desperate and ignorant in the world. The Jesuit mode of life is one of the many, many ways in which that grace can lift up a human being to companionship with almighty God.

Ignatius had received from his Divine Master an assurance that the Society he founded would always suffer persecution. He expressly directed his disciples to avoid any sort of conduct which would unnecessarily turn people against them. But if such persecution were to come without the Jesuits' own fault, he would welcome it as a sign that they were walking in the footsteps of the rejected and crucified Saviour. Sharing in Christ's shame (to use the language of the *Spiritual Exercises*), they and countless others to whom they had preached would share in the glory of His triumph. Ignatius' prophecy was abundantly fulfilled. Hardest to endure, most prolonged and vexing, were the attacks that came from inside the Church, from people who practiced or claimed to practice a rigorous piety. Or else they were Catholic rulers who found the Jesuits and their universal spirit of charity and their denunciation of crime in public places as inconvenient obstacles to their own autocratic and nationalistic ambitions. The *Monita Secreta* ("Secret Directives"), a canard against the Society, was published in Cracow by ex-Jesuits. It was reprinted hundreds of times—thirteen times in this country—and was responsible for an enormous amount of misinformation concerning the Society. From 1650 on, the controversy with the Jansenists on the nature and operations of divine grace, a dispute brought to a boiling point by Blaise Pascal's *Provincial Letters*, turned a large and influential part of Catholic opinion against the Jesuits.

Jesuits were employed in hospitals, as army chaplains, as promoters of vast charities. Ignatius himself, at the very outset of his religious career, had set an example of concern for social needs. Jesuits were confessors to kings and advisors of bishops. They engaged in popular parish missions on a vast scope, redeeming great areas of Europe from religious ignorance and unbelief by their preaching, confessions, and their high personal example. Some were employed for far-reaching diplomatic missions in the Church's service. Four of Ignatius' early companions were deputed to aid the bishops assembled in the Council of Trent. They engaged in a prodigious amount of literary and scientific activity, one of their principal achievements in the intellectual defense of Catholicism. One of the most authentic estimates of the Society's literary output (Sommervogel's *Bibliothèque des Écrivains de la Compagnie de Jésus* [*Bruxelles-Paris*, 1890–1909]), placed the total Jesuit production at 18,000 works, at the least.

Outside the foreign missions, the most striking of all the Society's achievements lay in the field of education: the great galaxy of schools that it soon called into being and continued to develop throughout its history. The original charter of the Jesuits, which Pope Paul III gave to them in 1540, did not, it is true, speak of schools as such. It defined their functions in much wider terms, stating them as follows:

> To labor for the advancement of souls in Christian life and learning, and for the spread of the Christian faith by public preaching and the ministry of God's word, by spiritual exercises and works of charity, more particularly by grounding boys and unlettered persons in Christianity.

Two facts, however, were prophetic of the part in education which the Jesuits were soon to play. The first fact is that the ten founding Fathers were all schoolmen, all university trained, and possessed the master of arts degree from the University of Paris which authorized them "to teach anywhere." The other fact was that new schools were being founded everywhere, and existing schools were being reorganized. It was a time of humanistic revival, and of religious revolt, and new issues confronted people's minds: so that the first Jesuits were soon besieged with invitations to start schools. In a short time, on April 24, 1548, under very favorable auspices they opened a school at Messina, in Sicily. A second school was opened in Sicily the following year, at Palermo, and thirty-five more schools were started within the next six years in eight European countries. At the end of twenty-five years the schools numbered 150, and almost exactly fifty years after the dedication of the first school at Messina, the Jesuits were conducting 245 educational institutions, not alone in Europe, but in India, Japan, Cuba, Mexico, and the Philippines as well. It is probable that history provides no similar expansion achieved in so short a time by a single organization. Most of the schools were of the type the French call a *lycée,* the Germans a *Gymnasium.* Only about one-third admitted boarders. They were generous, especially in Germany, in providing for charity students.

At least half these 245 schools had both secondary and collegiate departments, and about fifteen of them had a university status besides. Enrollments were significant. Very few of them had less than five hundred students, a considerable number had enrollment of more than a thousand, and not a few were near the two thousand mark. How was it possible for the internal development of the early Jesuit schools to keep pace with their rapid extension? The answer was provided by the appointment of an international superintendent of Jesuit schools, whose job it was to visit the existing Jesuit schools, organize and unify curricula, adjust personnel problems, plan further expansion of educational facilities, and deal with municipal, state, and ecclesiastical authorities.

The Jesuits fought in all parts of the far-flung battle line of the Catholic Restoration. They saved southern and western Germany, Hungary, Bohemia, Poland, and Belgium to the Faith: they led the papal cause in France; they strengthened the Catholic minorities in the dark hour of persecution in Holland, England, and Scotland; they helped in the preservation of Catholicism in Ireland.*

Through their innumerable enterprises in the field of scholarship—divine and secular, their belles-lettres and drama, their unwearied preaching and teaching, their skilled and voluminous "relations" or reports from mission lands, they made inestimable contributions to the culture of Christian countries, laid the seeds for many of the bold enterprises of modern thought and research, and interpreted to Western civilization the cultural wealth of the vast non-Christian world. Yet none of these activities prevented them from experiencing the hardest blow that could possibly befall them. In 1773 the Order was suppressed by Pope Clement XIV (Ganganelli) throughout the world. This terrible calamity came to them at the height of their development. In 1770 the

* Martin P. Harney, S.J., *The Jesuits in History* (New York, America Press, 1941), p. 191.

Society numbered 42 provinces, 24 houses of Professed Fathers, 669 colleges, 61 novitiates, 3,325 residences, 274 mission stations, and about 23,000 members, of whom 23 were in the United States in the Maryland Mission.

The basic cause of the Society's suppression was terrific political pressure, including a threat of large-scale seizure of papal territory, placed upon the Pope by the rulers of the various traditionally Catholic countries of Europe, and particularly by King Charles III of Spain, who blamed the Jesuits for riots. All these Governments had come strongly under the influence of the socially and politically destructive ideas that led to the horrors of the French Revolution. The combined onslaught upon the Order had been built up through the eighteenth century by the systematic circulation of a galaxy of anti-Jesuit literature, above and underground, much of it with completely fantastic accusations, not unlike, in our own times, the myths circulated about the Jews under the title "Protocols of the Elders of Zion." Wholesale dissolution by the Spanish Government under Charles III of the fifty-seven marvelous Jesuit missions, or "reductions," in Paraguay and the actions of the rabidly anticlerical government of Portugal under Pombal, had already set the pattern for dissolving the Jesuits as a body.

On the other hand, the *manner* of the suppression was curiously unique in the history of the Church. No grave misconduct was proved against the Society; the Pope's immediate predecessor, Pope Clement XIII, had issued a document highly commending the Jesuits against their critics. The document of suppression—the papal Brief, *Dominus ac Redemp-*

tor, July 21, 1773—was not self-operative: it took effect only when gradually promulgated in the respective dioceses or administrative regions of the Church. In two European countries—the Empire of Russia and the Kingdom of Prussia— the respective rulers refused to allow its proclamation, although neither of these rulers was Catholic; indeed, Empress Catherine II of Russia was violently opposed to the Catholic Church and the Pope! Hence it was that the Society continued a sort of token existence in these two countries, and after 1780 in Russia alone, with the tacit approval of Pius VI (1774–99). When the Jesuits in Russia met and elected a Vicar General on October 17, 1782, Pope Pius VI orally approved their action. Pius VII, his successor (1800–23), gave formal approval to the Society in Russia on March 7, 1801. In the British colonies and in Maryland Jesuits regrouped to prepare for the restoration of the Society.

American ex-Jesuits had stayed quietly on their property in Maryland and Pennsylvania, changing little of their traditional religious life. Finally, in 1805, Pope Pius VII gave permission to re-affiliate with the relics of the "Old Society" in Prussia and Russia, and on August 7, 1814, restored the Order for the whole world, with Father Thaddeus Brzozowski (1805–20) as General.

The third General of the restored Society, Father Johannes Roothaan, a Dutchman (1829–53), began its revival by a thorough study of the original text of the *Exercises.* The Jesuits went bravely ahead, profiting by the lessons of the past, and building up from a humble and solid foundation.

Today, as of January 1, 1955, there are 32,899 members

of the Society of Jesus in the world, some of whom are still imprisoned behind the Iron Curtain. The Society is divided for administrative purposes into eight main divisions or Assistancies: Italian, German, French, Spanish, English, American, Slavic, and Latin American. Each of these contains a number of provinces or vice-provinces. The province is the unit of government in the Society, under the head of the entire body—the Father General, who is elected for life by the General Congregation, composed of delegates from the provinces, and resides permanently in Rome. The present Father General is the Very Reverend John B. Janssens, a Belgian by nationality. The Fathers Assistant (or Assistants as they are popularly called) are also elected by the General Congregation for life and also reside in Rome at the Jesuit world headquarters, Borgo Santo Spirito 5, near the Vatican. The present American Assistant is Father Vincent A. McCormick, a New Yorker. All other officials of the Society are appointed either by the Father General, who retains supreme power, or by the several provincials within their own jurisdiction.

Largest of all the Assistancies is the American, with a total of 7,751 members. There are 4,204 priests and 2,919 scholastics (that is, young members preparing for the priesthood), and 628 coadjutor brothers. The total includes Americans studying abroad or working in the American-manned foreign missions, and is distributed among ten provinces and one dependent vice-province.

Father Louis de Quiroz, S.J., and the catechists Gabriel de Solis and Juan Bautista Solis, were slain by Indians in Virginia on February 4, 1571. Father Juan Bautista de Segura, S.J., the catechist Cristóbal Redondo, and Brothers Gabriel Gómez, Pedro Linores, and Sancho Cevallos were slain five days later.

The Jesuit mission of Nouvelle France began on June 12, 1611, when Fathers Biard and Massé arrived at Port Royal, Canada. The first settlement of white men in New England was that of the Jesuits at Mount Desert Island, Maine. Father Isaac Jogues, a missionary to the Hurons, entered the present New York State in 1642 as a prisoner of the Mohawks. Two years later, in 1644, Father Bressani, while on his way to the Huron missions, was captured by the Mohawks, tortured like Father Jogues, then sold to the Dutch and transported back to France. During the days of May, 1646, Father Jogues paid a brief visit as an ambassador of good will to his torturers in New York State. Between 1642 and 1649 occurred the death of the eight French missionaries to the Iroquois and Huron Indians, known as the North American Martyrs, whose feast the Church in the United States celebrates annually on September 26. Five of these (St. John de Brébeuf and his companions) were tortured and died near the present Midland, Ontario, in Canada. Three (St. Isaac Jogues and his companions, the coadjutors John Lalande and René Goupil), experienced a like fate at Auriesville, near Schenectady, in New York State. Both Midland and Auriesville are today much-frequented places of pilgrimage and of spiritual retreats.

Though the French Jesuit missionaries continued for a

time in New York State, the French Government officially abandoned the Iroquois mission field in 1687, and the English obliged them to withdraw. Some, however, continued to come to New York State until 1708.

In the records of Trinity Church (Protestant Episcopal) in New York City, the writer came upon a report submitted to the Reverend Rector of Trinity Church, at the dawn of the eighteenth century, by a French Huguenot catechist whom Trinity Parish employed as a missionary to the Negroes and Indians. The report concerned the state of religion in the Royal Colony of Connecticut, and was rather discouraged in tone. The Jesuits (that is to say, French Jesuits from Canada) were, he said, imparting their superstitions to the Indians, and to make it worse were living like the Indians, dwelling with them in their wigwams. The Jesuits experienced such poverty that one of them did not even have a shirt to his back. He had applied to the Royal Governor Bellomont for the gift of a shirt, and the Governor simply bawled him out and told him to leave the country. Though the catechist did not approve of what the Jesuit Father was teaching, he thought the Governor had acted wrongly. Indeed, he thought such a brave man deserved the present of a dozen shirts. However, there were greater threats than the Jesuits—namely, the Quakers, who were insinuating themselves everywhere. One Quaker, explained the catechist, can do more spiritual damage than a dozen Jesuits. A good Quaker friend of mine to whom I told this story found that it cheered him no end: he had always been under the impression that nobody could ever get ahead of a Jesuit. Whatever be the merits in that particular instance, the missionaries whom the Huguenot catechist found living in wigwams in Connecticut were just another instance of the spirit the Jesuit missions cherished from the start: to live close to the people you were working for, share their life and their hardships, and speak to them in the language of our common humanity.

In the Southwest, Father Juan Maria Salvatierra began his mission work in 1697. Together with Father Eusebio Kino, Jacobo Sedlmayr, and Wenceslao Link, they crossed the peninsula of Lower California and strung out a broken line of widely separated missions along its inner shore. Father Kino, the indefatigable "Padre on horseback," did mission work in the present United States, including St. Xavier del Bac in Arizona.

The Maryland-Pennsylvania mission is the source to which the Catholic Church in the United States traces its origin as an organized, hierarchical body. The mission began on March 25, 1634, with the arrival of Father Andrew White, an English Jesuit, and his two companions, Father Altham and Brother Gervase, to Lord Baltimore's Maryland colony, and lasted as a Jesuit institution until 1773, the year of the Society's suppression.

In November, 1633, Father White was appointed to accompany Lord Baltimore's expedition, and after a three months' voyage arrived at the mouth of the Potomac River. Immediately on arrival, Father White celebrated the first Mass in Maryland on St. Clement's Island, near Leonardtown. For eleven years he labored among the Indians of Maryland and the surrounding country. His mention of the Indians in his famous *Relatio Itineris,* or description of the colonists' voyage from England to Maryland, is one of the few authentic records left of the Susquehannas, the Patuxents, and the Piscataways. Father White founded a mission among the Piscataways. By patient study he mastered the language of the tribes among whom he worked and prepared for them a catechism, grammar, and vocabulary in their own language. On July 5, 1641, he baptized the chief of the tribe and his squaw in a little chapel of birch bark built for that purpose. The Governor, his council, and many of the colonists attended the ceremony. In the afternoon the couple were united in Christian matrimony and a great cross was planted.

In 1645 the kindly rule established by Lord Baltimore in Maryland was overthrown by the Virginian adventurer Clayborne. Father White was seized, put in chains, and sent to England, where for a time he was confined in prison and then banished. Unable to return to Maryland, he succeeded in returning to England and labored for the conversion of his countrymen another ten years, always under the penalty of death which was incurred by any priest who re-entered the country after banishment. He died on December 27, 1656, revered by all who knew him as a great missionary, scholar, and saint.

Through long years of bitter persecution the Jesuit missionaries in Maryland and their devoted followers managed to survive. As early as 1704 Jesuits from Maryland went north into Pennsylvania. In 1734, Father Joseph Greaton opened a chapel for about forty Catholics in Philadelphia, at the spot which is now Old St. Joseph's Church (Willing's Alley). German Jesuits came to the fore with German settlers. However, what the Puritans and later the Episcopalians had not been able to do was finally accomplished in 1773 by the Catholic kings of Europe. At the time of the Suppression, there were in Maryland and Pennsylvania twenty-three Jesuits, and scattered Catholics.

In the Maryland colony the Suppression meant the corporate disbanding of its twenty-three Jesuits but not the cessation of their ministries. Even after the promulgation of the fatal Brief, twenty fathers remained at their Maryland and Pennsylvania mission posts, continuing to labor as secular priests and even to found new missions. In the immediate sequel of the abolition of the Society, England lost her colonies, and in the new political and social order of things, Pope Pius VI erected the See of Baltimore. As its first bishop the Sovereign Pontiff appointed one of the ex-Jesuits, John Carroll, under whose jurisdiction came the entire territory of the United States and his disbanded brethren of the Maryland Mission as well.

For these remnants, a brighter day dawned with the opening of the new century. In 1791, twenty-seven years after the Brief of Suppression, rumors crossed the ocean that Pope Pius VII had legalized the existence of the Order in White Russia (now called Byelorussia), and that authority was given to the General to aggregate members in other countries. Death had by this time sadly thinned the ranks of the original disbanded Maryland Fathers. Inquiry confirmed the reports. At St. Thomas' Manor in Charles County, Maryland, a few former Jesuits, surviving after the Suppression in 1773, re-entered the

Society on August 18, 1805, when it was privately restored by papal authority in what by this time was the United States Federal Union. On that occasion a decree from the Vicar General in Russia, Father Gabriel Gruber, was read to the assembled ex-Jesuits in the spacious upper hall of St. Thomas Manor, appointing Father Robert Molyneux as superior of the revived Maryland mission, with powers to establish a novitiate for the training of new recruits, and to govern the missionary contingent.

Most Americans in our nation on wheels visit the National Capital at some time during their lives. If you are tired of trudging around Capitol Hill and Constitution Avenue, and the weather is tolerable, take Route 301 that leads directly south through Charles County, Maryland, and the Morgantown Bridge over the Potomac River into Virginia and points beyond. If you leave the main highway to the right a few miles beyond La Plata, Charles County's capital, at a spot called Bel Alton, the Chapel Point road will bring you shortly to stately old St. Ignatius Church, built by Archbishop John Carroll in 1798. Adjacent is an equally stately colonial brick residence—St. Thomas Manor House. Save for the part of the house destroyed by fire in 1866 and restored, the building dates from 1741. From its broad windows and from the beautiful churchyard, you look out over the vast sweep of the lower Potomac and its tributary, Port Tobacco Creek. The old Jesuit manor property, which you see below the hill and across the creek, dates from the very foundation of the Maryland Colony in 1634. In earlier days folks came in sailboats and rowboats to Mass from across the water. The Jesuit manor property in Maryland and Pennsylvania (Conewago) is one of the few present Jesuit properties in the world which date from the early days of the Society. It was kept intact by the associated ex-Jesuits during the years of the Suppression. Its thirty-nine farms have been managed for many years on a carefully elaborated plan, highly advantageous to the tenants, by Brother William E. Carley, S.J., one of the most skilled and humanely knowledgeable Irish-born agriculturists you are ever likely to meet.

A visit to St. Thomas Manor will recall these events, and the part played in the early history of the Catholic Church in this country by the Jesuits, or former Jesuits, in a long line of missionaries, either in Maryland or radiating from it into nearby Virginia, Pennsylvania, Delaware, and even New York. St. Thomas Manor is one of the three earliest centers of this old Maryland-Pennsylvania mission, the other two being New-town Manor, near Leonardtown, in St. Mary's County, Maryland, and St. Inigoes Manor, near the southern extremity of St. Mary's County. The Newtown Manor house is still intact. Only a fragment of the St. Inigoes house remains, and this is on Government property (Webster Airfield), but the eighteenth-century St. Inigoes Manor church of St. Ignatius has been restored as a shrine.

At the time of the general restoration of the Society which was decreed by Pope Pius VII on August 17, 1814, there were only three survivors in the United States of the ancient Jesuits: Father Charles Neale, who had re-entered the Society, and two other Marylanders, John Carroll, Archbishop of Baltimore since 1798, and his coadjutor, Bishop Leonard Neale. By that same date, there were already fifty Jesuits with headquarters at Georgetown in the District of Columbia. Their number grew steadily during the next two decades. When, in 1833, the membership of the mission had increased to ninety and the houses to thirteen, Father General Roothaan, by decree of February 2, 1833, constituted the American mission into a full-fledged province which would now move forward by its own power.

The Jesuits then were located as follows: District of Columbia—Georgetown College; Maryland—White Marsh (novitiate), Frederick, St. Thomas, St. Inigoes, Newtown, Bohemia, and St. Joseph; Pennsylvania—Conewago, Goshenhoppen, Paradise, Lancaster, Philadelphia; Virginia—Alexandria.

The eighty charter members of 1833 had by 1878 grown to 293 busy men engaged in study, teaching, and in every phase of the ministry in six states. The house had multiplied from thirteen to twenty-three. In 1832 French Jesuits, who came to Kentucky in 1830, took charge of St. Mary's College, near Bardstown; this college was transferred in 1846 from Kentucky to New York, and settled at Fordham. In 1852, operating from the Church of St. Francis Xavier on Sixteenth Street as a center, the New York Fathers undertook the spiritual ministrations among the unfortunates of the city jails, hospitals, asylums, and almshouses situated on the East River islands, from Blackwell's (now Welfare) to Harts, which ministrations they are still carrying on, with seven Fathers permanently engaged in this work of mercy.

A Report on the American Jesuits

The Jesuits in Mid-America, 1673–1763

Less written about, less generally known, but projected upon an immense scale of territory, effort, and time is the story of the Jesuit pioneers in the Midwestern area of our country. On April 11, 1823, a little band of Jesuits left the recently established Maryland Jesuit novitiate at White Marsh, Maryland, to travel to distant Missouri at the invitation of the Bishop of St. Louis, the Most Rev. W. V. Du Bourg, to work for both white settlers and Indians. The band consisted of two Belgian Fathers, Charles Van Quickenborne and P. J. Timmermans, three coadjutor brothers, seven Belgian novices, and six Negro slaves from the old Maryland plantations. A home and center of operations was provided for them at the property of St. Ferdinand de Florissant, outside St. Louis (near which, in 1819, the Blessed Mother Philippine Duchesne had begun the foundation of the Religious of the Sacred Heart in this country).*

The arrival of Father Van Quickenborne and his Belgian novices at Florissant in 1823 marked the renewal, after a period of forced interruption, rather than the actual beginning of Jesuit missionary enterprise in the Middle United States. That beginning was made at least as early as 1673 when Father Marquette in his historic voyage down the Mississippi ministered to the Indians along its banks and formed plans for evangelizing the region drained by the great waterway and its tributary streams. These plans were to be realized, if not

* Cf. Gilbert Garraghan, S.J., *The Jesuits of the Middle United States* (3 vols.; New York, America Press, 1938). Many items in this section are taken from Father Garraghan's scholarly work.

wholly, at least in part. The work of religious and humanitarian service in behalf of the native red men inaugurated by Marquette was carried forward in the face of tremendous obstacles by successive members of his order, Mid-America remaining a favorite field of Jesuit missionary activity down to 1773, when, as an incident in the general destruction of the Society of Jesus throughout the world, its missions in that section of North America were struck down at a single blow.

Between Marquette, the first Jesuit to traverse the watershed of the Mississippi, and Sebastian Louis Meurin, the last of his eighteenth-century successors to exercise the sacred ministry in that region, a long line of missionaries of the Society of Jesus devoted themselves to the formidable task of Christianizing and civilizing the savage population of mid-continental North America. It would not be in accord with the facts to say that their labors issued in complete success. Difficulties of every description were met with, thwarting their pious designs and preventing them from reaping in proper measure the fruits of the harvest. But the work was nobly planned and heroically persevered in, and its written record, as we read it in the letters of Gravier, Gabriel Marest, Vivier, and their associates, is a fascinating chapter in the history of Catholic missionary achievement in the New World.

The group of Belgian Jesuits that settled on the banks of the Missouri in the third decade of the nineteenth century were therefore not the first of their Order to enter the great sweep of territory flanked by the Alleghanies and the Rockies. A path for civilization, no less than for the Gospel, had been blazed before them by their brethren of the seventeenth and eighteenth centuries. Since grateful personal recollections of the earlier line of Jesuit workers still lingered in the memory of the oldest inhabitants when Van Quickenborne and his party appeared on the scene, the thread of continuity between the old and the new Society of Jesus in the Middle United States remained in a sense unbroken. For example, on November 16, 1810, the Trappist Dom Urban Guillet communicated to Bishop Carroll a petition on the part of the people of the "Illinois country" for a Jesuit missionary. It reads in part as follows:

> Last Sunday we were visited here by a venerable old man with whom I had a long talk in French. He had lived with our Fathers on the missions among the savages and was now transacting some private business with the Government. For fifty years he lived with the Illinois, the Iroquois, the Hurons, and others, among whom our Fathers Lalemant, Jogues and others were slain. When the missions had ceased upon the death of our Fathers, he himself used to baptize the children of the Indians and collect them into his house on Sundays for instruction. "It was a pleasure," he said, "to hear with what affection they used to speak of their Fathers." However, his business affairs forced him to leave them and they were deprived of all help. Not long since he journeyed through their country and visited them. They brought him to an island and showed him there on a rock some blood which could not be washed away. It was the blood of a Father whose name I have forgotten, but who was killed by the Indians in the last days of the old Society. The murderers, they told him, had all met with a wretched and unhappy death. They were very anxious to have the Fathers with them. The English Governor (for some, though not all, live in parts subject to the English) sent them Protestant ministers. They were asked whether they had wives, and when they replied that they had, the Indians said:

Graveyard of pioneer American Jesuits, St. Stanislaus Seminary, Florissant, Mo.

Gravestone of Father Peter de Smet.

"Our black gowns who were with us before had no wives."
They sent word, therefore, to the Governor that they would
like to have the holy Jesuit priests.*

Two years after the establishment of St. Louis University in
1829, a delegation of the Rocky Mountain Indians came to St.
Louis to ask for a "black robe" to go back with them. Their
ancestors had been converts to Catholicism some 150 years before in New York and Canada. Now having been forced into
the Rockies by the white man, they remembered the days of
the "black robes" as happy and tranquil days. In 1831 there
were no Jesuits to go back with them, but as they kept sending down delegations, the Jesuits finally sent Father Peter de
Smet in answer to their request. In the next thirty-odd years
De Smet traveled over 200,000 miles in the interest of the red
men, who were being pushed further and further back. During the Civil War, when most of the troops had been with-
drawn from the frontier to fight in the south, De Smet kept
the natives calm. Later, when a punitive expedition was sent
against them, he refused to go, but in 1868 he went along
among the Sioux in South Dakota, who were under the leadership of Sitting Bull, and persuaded them to send representatives to a peace commission where a treaty was signed.

At mid-century, the Midwestern Jesuits of the United States
are conducting establishments in Missouri, Kansas, Nebraska,
South Dakota, Wyoming, Colorado, Minnesota, Wisconsin,
Michigan, Ohio, Indiana, and Illinois, and also in British
Honduras and British East India (now India and Pakistan).
Moreover, they have in the past maintained houses in Louisi-

* Baltimore Archdiocesan Archives.

ana and Kentucky and in the territory now comprised within the states of Montana, Idaho, Washington, and Oregon. Their present field of operation may be said to comprise in the rough two great regions; one, the part of the basin of the Great Lakes lying south of the Canadian border and west of New York State, the other the upper Mississippi Valley, exclusive of its extreme northwestern reaches.* The first Jesuit name to be associated with the upper Great Lakes is that of St. Isaac Jogues, who, in 1641, in company with Father Charles Raymbault, planted the cross at Sault Ste. Marie in what is now the State of Michigan; the first Jesuit name to be distinctly connected with the Mississippi Valley is the historic one of Jacques Marquette, who with Louis Jolliet discovered the upper Mississippi River at Prairie du Chien, Wisconsin, June 17, 1673. With these memorable names, Jogues, the martyr-priest, and Marquette, the discoverer, begins the story of Jesuit activity in the great sweep of territory now cultivated by the Society of Jesus in the Middle United States.

No more engaging pages in history may be read than those that unfold the successive scenes in the gripping drama of discovery, exploration, and splendid pioneering enacted on the stage of Mid-America by the French of the seventeenth and eighteenth centuries. The theme has been handled repeatedly by the historians, notably by Francis Parkman in his classic volumes and by Clarence Walworth Alvord in his *Illinois Country*. Two sharply contrasted groups of participants divide the action between them; on the one hand, the empire

---

* The Jesuits of the lower Mississippi Valley are organized as a separate administrative unit with headquarters at New Orleans.

builders, the colonial officials of whatever grade, the fur traders, the adventurers by forest and stream, and the sparsely scattered habitants; on the other hand, the Church's representatives, more particularly the missionaries to the Indians, as the Franciscans and Jesuits, whose activities in evangelizing the native tribes of the New World are of lasting record.

The following are some of the old French Jesuit missionaries whose names are identified, since the seventeenth and eighteenth centuries, with the territory of so many of the Midwestern states.

Michigan: Fathers Menard, Marquette, and Dablon.

Wisconsin: Father Claude Allouez, who wrote about the Illinois Indians.

Illinois: Father Marquette, who was present at the opening of the site that later became Chicago, and at Kaskaskia, on the Mississippi. The story of his 1673 expedition is the earliest account of the river. The Jesuits established a mission in the heart of Chicago from 1696 to 1702. They were the first large-scale wheat growers and the earliest school teachers in that region.

Missouri: St. Louis and St. Genevieve. Father Sebastian Meurin was the first priest to attend Laclède's settlement of St. Louis. They dealt with many important Indian tribes, and discovered and described the Missouri River.

Iowa: Father Marquette and his companions were the first white men on its soil.

Minnesota: In 1727, Father Michael Grignas established the Sioux mission of St. Michael the Archangel. Father Jean-Pierre Aul was slain June 5, 1736.

Indiana: The Jesuits were the first white men among the Miamis.

Ohio: The oldest Catholic establishment in the limits of the state was the Jesuit Wyandot mission on the Sandusky River, about 1751. Father Joseph-Pierre de Bonnécamp labored there around 1749. The oldest map of Ohio's boundaries yet discovered was made by a Jesuit missionary.

For over a hundred years the Jesuits had striven in that vast territory to uplift the Indians and redeem the terrible record of the white man's greed and cruelty. But France's Superior Council of June 9, 1763, decreed the destruction of the work of all Jesuits under its jurisdiction. The decree was abruptly and harshly executed Last to serve was the venerable Father Sebastien L. Meurin, who died of a broken heart on February 23, 1777, and was laid to rest in the historic graveyard at Florissant, Missouri.

In the Deep South, the Jesuit missionaries of the early nineteenth century had to face a very different enemy than Indians and their tomahawks. French Jesuits opened the College of Grand-Côteau in the Evangeline country of southwestern Louisiana in 1837. In 1848, they inaugurated a college, later Loyola University of the South, in New Orleans. But the dread scourge of cholera decimated them in 1848, and for thirty years, from 1848 to 1878, they were constantly threatened with the plague of yellow fever. From their earliest origins, the Jesuits had always made a special point of active care for the plague-stricken, losing thereby the lives of many of their members, and the tradition cost them many lives in the New Orleans mission.

From Italy, on the other hand, came most of the Jesuit missionary pioneers of the West Coast, the Rockies, and the Northwest. Jesuits from the province of Rome and Turin were pioneers in California, Oregon, and Washington. The Alaska missions were also largely pioneered by Italians, many of them men of great culture. The first permanent Jesuit major seminary in the United States, founded near Baltimore in 1869, was staffed in part by such scholars as the astronomer Secchi, the theologians Mazella (later Cardinal Mazella) and De Augustinis, and the political analyst Brandi.

PART TWO

MISSION

THE TRAINING OF JESUITS

Seminarian's desk in ascetory, or study-hall, at Shadowbrook, Lenox, Mass., before fire which occurred in winter, 1956.

Novices at humble tasks in the kitch-
en, while a fellow-novice reads aloud.

Master of Novices conducting a class in Greek at Shadowbrook.

First Vows

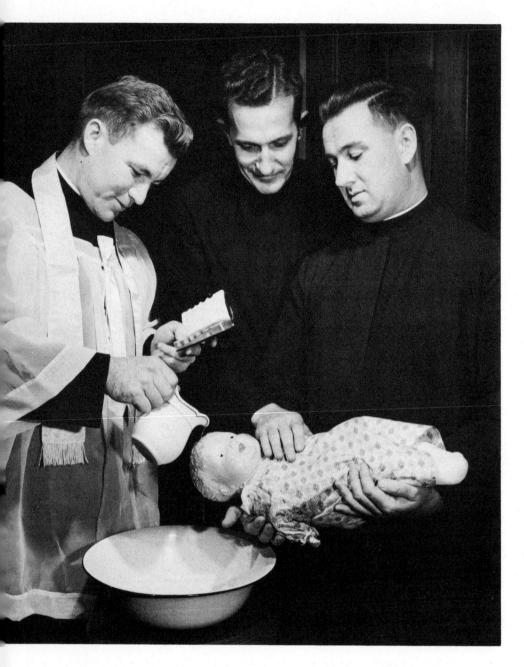

Practicing baptism on doll used for 26 years at Weston
College and known to scholastics as "Bertha Quaedam."

THE TRAINING OF JESUITS

M ISS Bourke-White's photographs are taken at each of
the principal stages in a Jesuit's training, so let us
review the steps quickly in order.

The young candidate for the Society begins his career as a
novice from the moment he sets foot inside a Jesuit novitiate,
or "House of Probation," as it is officially called. At once he
starts to follow the simple daily order that will continue, sub-
stantially, for the rest of his life. For American Jesuits this
means rising at 5:30 A.M., a brief visit to the chapel followed
by an hour's private meditation, Mass at 7 o'clock, followed

by breakfast and a round of duties through the day and evening until retiring at 10 P.M. After a couple of weeks—somewhat longer if he is a candidate for the status of coadjutor brother—the novice starts to wear the black cassock, the home dress of all the Catholic clergy who do not wear some distinctive Order habit.

Close to the beginning of his noviceship—the two-year period during which the candidate studies the Society and the Society studies him—the novice makes a thirty-day retreat: the full schedule of the *Exercises* of St. Ignatius. He learns the meaning of those daily practices that form part of the routine of his daily life: meditation, examens, litanies, spiritual reading, and so on. Much of his time during the two-year period is taken up with humble labor, indoors and outdoors, following the example of Jesus our Lord at Nazareth. Regular periods of prayer and of study punctuate the program. The novice learns to know the Rules and the Constitution of the Order, and he also improves his knowledge of ancient and modern languages, history, and the other academic disciplines. Educational standards for those who enter the Society are increasingly high.

The novice, like novices in all religious communities, is never left to himself. He lives in close association with his fellow novices, studying with them in a common study hall, and joining with them in the games and recreation that are necessary to keep a young man alert and in good physical trim. The daily order is broken up into a multitude of small duties, all of them fitting into a general pattern of fraternal life and a quiet progress in the spirit of simplicity and detachment from selfish interests. He is under the continual guidance, too, of the novitiate's director, the Master of Novices, who is friend, father, and counsellor. His time of early probation comes to an end when, on the morning that follows the second anniversary of his day of entrance, he pronounces to his superior, during Mass, before receiving Holy Communion, the three simple but perpetual vows of poverty, chastity, and obedience. Once these vows are taken, he ranks as a Jesuit scholastic, and writes "S. J." after his name.

His years as a scholastic are spent in four main periods. As a so-called "Junior," he applies himself for two years directly after the noviceship in acquiring for himself some of the liberal-arts knowledge he will require as a future teacher of youth. Standard topics in the Juniorate period (which is usually spent in a separate wing of the novitiate building) are Latin, Greek, English, history—ancient and modern, mathematics. Much attention is paid, in accordance with Jesuit tradition, to the art and method of self-expression, both in writing and in speech. The studies lead up to the degree of bachelor of arts (if that has not already been acquired). With the development of modern library science, young American Jesuits are encouraged to make ample use of the best library facilities available.

Juniorate finished—or in some cases shortened or even omitted, where a man is already academically advanced—the next step is three years as a "Philosopher" in one of the Order's seminaries or scholasticates. These in the United States are as follows: Woodstock, Md. (theology); Weston, Mass. (theology and philosophy); Shrub Oak, N. Y. (philosophy);

71

Spring Hill, Ala. (philosophy); West Baden, Ind. (philosophy); St. Mary's, Kansas (theology); St. Louis, Mo. (philosophy); Spokane, Wash. (philosophy); Alma, Calif. (theology). These are years of introduction to the great thinkers: Aristotle, Plato, Augustine, Thomas Aquinas, Suarez, and their successors, commentators, and adversaries. It is a time when a man learns to ponder over the eternal questions of Being and Change, the One and the Many, Creator and Creature, Soul and Body, Essence and Existence, Knowledge and Reality, Freedom and Necessity, ultimate Right and Wrong; to learn the great story of how minds have wrestled with these topics, for better or for worse, since the dawn of civilization. Expensive laboratory equipment sets the introduction to the intricacies of scientific method and discovery. Further study is made of speech and communication. It is the time of hard, scholarly labor spent in an atmosphere of peace and friendship. Particularly in these Philosophy years many a Jesuit writer or scholar lays the foundations for his future research or expression.

The life of a Jesuit scholastic during his Philosophy years does not offer a striking contrast with that of any seminarian preparing for the priesthood in the Catholic Church, all of whom are obliged today to spend at least two years of philosophy before they can pass on to the theological course. But at the close of the philosophy period, Ignatius introduces his men directly to the apostolate without waiting for them to become priests. Suddenly, after from five to eight years of complete severance from the great world around them, they are thrown out into the busy classroom, and for another three years (in a period called the "Regency") the scholastics teach any of the four years of high school. Later in this story I indicate something of what this means in the life of the boys themselves. It is equally educative in the life of the young religious, for he comes immediately into contact with the busy, live world of active youth: their ambitions and troubles, their virtues and waywardness, their schemes and interests and sports, their spiritual difficulties and their vocations. It is a school of humanity, taught by humanity itself—very human humanity with no holds barred. At the same time, the little world of the school's extracurricular activities, from the school monthly magazine to the glee club, dramatic society, or local radio program, are often a prelude to the apostolic activities of later life.

The Regency period is not always spent in teaching. For some men it is a time for special studies, in the United States or abroad; or for acquiring special university degrees, either in our Catholic schools or in some of the major secular institutions.

In any case, after his Regency the Jesuit aspirant returns to the quiet of the cloister, to begin his four years of theological study proper, as a much more mature individual than the young Philosopher who packed his grip one August morning and anxiously, but hopefully, entered the theater of his Regency activities. He has learned and usually profited from a firsthand experience of American youth in the classroom, chapel, and place of recreation.

In his Philosophy years, the aspirant made reflective acquaintance with some of the thought of great minds concerning the problems of God's creation. In the four years of Theology, he studies the methods and channels by which the

Creator has revealed His wisdom to the creature, and the reflections and analyses that man, under the guidance of the Holy Spirit, has made upon this Revelation in return. Dogmatic and patristic theology, moral theology, apologetics, canon law, Scripture—Old and New Testament—and its interpretation, Church history, and liturgy are the main topics for the Theology years. The priesthood is no longer a distant goal, but a matter for immediate preparation; and in the Jesuit course, Holy Orders are conferred at the end of three years of Theology, so that the fourth year of the theological course is made by men—"Fourth Year Fathers"—who are already ordained priests.

Preparation for the priesthood is practical as well as theoretical. The theologian learns the rites of the Church by actual rehearsal, and completes his preparation by a course in pastoral theology. In some of the theology schools the students conduct correspondence courses in theology with distant inquirers.

After so many years of preparation, the moment of ordination is a particularly solemn and moving event, whether it takes place in the seminary chapel or in a cathedral. The first thought of the newly ordained priest is to confer his priestly blessing upon his nearest and dearest, if any of them are present, and upon his own brethren in the Society, young and old alike. This event is followed by his first Holy Mass, usually said privately in the scholasticate, without special ceremony, followed shortly after by his first solemn or sung Mass, often celebrated in his own parish church at home.

Yet even then, a year after ordination, when the four years of theology have been completed and all examinations passed, the preparation is not yet completed. One more year remains: a period known as the "Third Probation" or "Tertianship." Those who are engaged in it are known as the "Tertian Fathers" or simply "Tertians." Knowing the peculiarities of intellectual men as he did, and living in a university atmosphere, Ignatius' mind was troubled by the drying or withering effect that long study is apt to effect in men's hearts unless there is something to counterbalance it. In the long search after knowledge, men are inclined to lose sight of the elementary goals that so moved their feelings and inspired their chivalry at the beginning of their religious career. In the scrutiny of trees, one can lose sight of the forest itself. Hence at the end of the long and weary course, the cautious Founder, as it were, exclaimed: "Wait a bit before you get under way with your busy life! Let's return to the sources of your first love. Let's renew that deep self-examination that moved you so effectively in your far-off noviceship days. You will spend one more year, in still more complete retirement, at a School of the Heart *(Schola Affectus),* as these long years have been a School of the Intellect."

During the Tertianship, therefore, spent in a separate residence exclusively devoted to that purpose, those who have completed their courses of training make the full thirty-day retreat for the second time in their career. The theory of the spiritual and the ascetic life, diverse methods of communicat-

ing the *Exercises,* certain practical aspects of the priest's ministry and preaching, and a systematic study of the Society's Constitutions or Institute form a major part of their time. An intensive return to the spirit and practice of contemplation,
according to the mind of Ignatius, is the most precious part of
this year, thus setting the pace for the remainder of their lives.
During the Lenten season the Tertians usually disperse, to
engage for the first time in the active ministry of preaching,
hearing confessions, caring for the sick in the hospitals, and so
forth, returning to the residence for Holy Week and its cere-
monies at home. The Tertianship lasts exactly ten months
and, at its expiration in the spring or early summer, the new
Jesuit priest receives his first "status" or appointment to the
new field of activity.

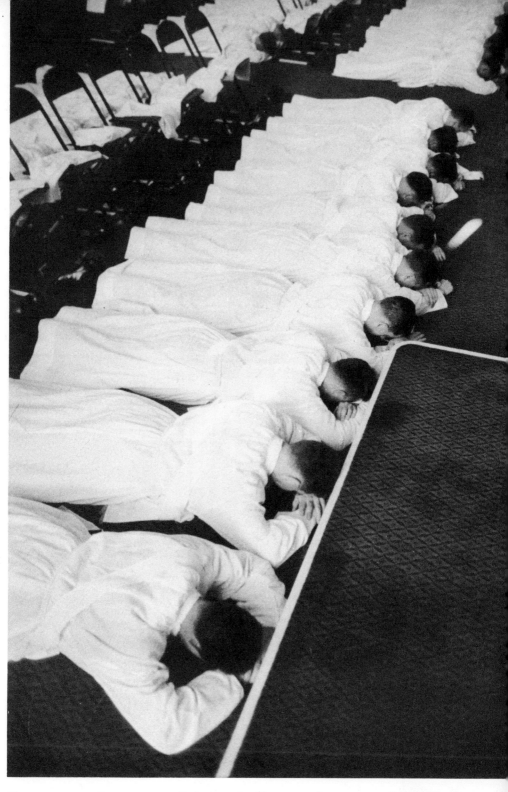

CEREMONY OF ORDINATION: Priests-to-be lie prone in gesture of humility.

Parents and close relatives at the moment of anointing.

The laying on of hands.

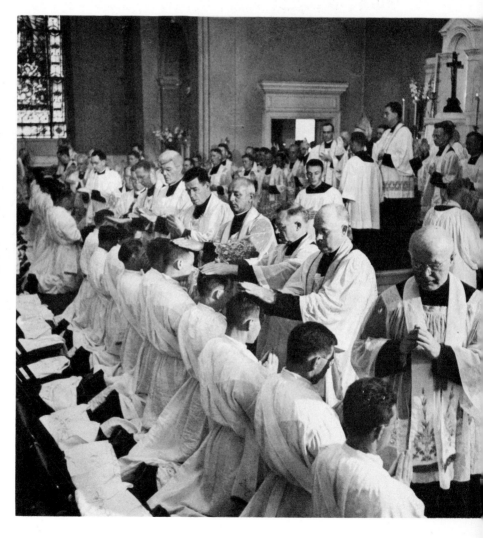

A newly ordained priest blessing and kissing his parents.

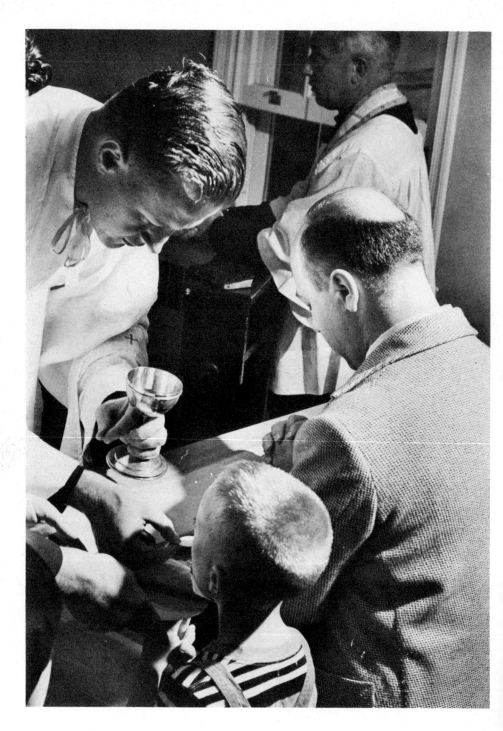

A first Mass.

The blessing of a new priest.

A young girl receives her priest-uncle's first blessing.

FACTS ON JESUIT EDUCATION
IN THE UNITED STATES

TO offer an over-all view of Jesuit educational activity
in the United States would be to compile a thick volume. In this short space, we can content ourselves with merely
a few simple statistics, figures that would have seemed incredible a century ago and, for the older members of the Order,
are hard to believe even today. The annual survey of Jesuit
education, published by the *Jesuit Educational Quarterly,* reports the following for January, 1955:

Jesuit schools have expanded at a rate proportional to the
expansion of education in the United States. From 1890 to

1950 the rate for the United States was 1,658.5%; for Jesuit schools it was 1,632.9%. During the last 75 years (1880-1954), Jesuit high school, college, and university enrollment have increased from 4,330 to 122,338.

The Jesuits conduct 33 colleges and universities in the United States, of which 6 are seminaries (scholasticates or houses of study for the Order members). Of these 33, 15 are colleges only, and 17 are universities, to which one must add Boston College (Chestnut Hill, Mass.). Despite its name, Boston College, with its harmonious Gothic university architecture, is a full-fledged university; but the title Boston University had long since been pre-empted by another institution.

These institutions imparted knowledge in 1954–55 to a total of 32,668 liberal arts students. Day courses in the commerce schools were followed by 9,707; night commerce courses by 8,952. Dentistry studies were pursued by 2,150 students; Divinity (that is to say, the theological courses) by 761, these latter being, with few exceptions, Jesuit seminarians. University and college courses in education enrolled 4,001, and engineering, 4,302—both of these popular specialties with students from distant colonial or former colonial countries, who hope to return to the land of their origin and help their countrymen with better schools and better living conditions.

In the graduate schools 2,148 followed the study of law by day and 1,840 by night. At the present time there are five schools of medicine in the Assistancy: at Georgetown University, Washington, D.C.; at Loyola University, Chicago (called the Cardinal Stritch School of Medicine); at Creighton University, Omaha; at Marquette University, Milwaukee, and

1,961; nursing claimed 3,422; pharmacy, 646; social welfare and social service, 522; and various miscellaneous graduate branches, 7,901. Among the latter we would include such unique institutions as the Parks School of Aeronautics at St. Louis University; Georgetown's Foreign Service School and School of Linguistics; Fordham University's Center for Russian Studies; Marquette's School of Journalism and School of Medical Technology; Loyola (Chicago) University's Institute of Social and Industrial Relations; and such fields as pre-clinical nursing and evening courses in liberal arts, music, dental technique, speech, physical therapy, besides short courses on labor law, adult education, adult opportunity, advertising, and more. And this list is by no means complete.

College and university students totaled 97,183, plus 15,013 veterans during 1954–55. In the Jesuit summer schools were enrolled 6,369 graduates and 17,791 undergraduates. To these add a total of 25,155 boys educated in American Jesuit high schools. The combined total enrollment of colleges, universities, and high schools is 122,338—an increase over the preceeding year of 5,952, or 5.1%. (The total U.S. college and university enrollment for this period was estimated at 2,078,-095. While 198,930 attended Catholic colleges of all kinds in the United States, some of these students were non-Catholics; and 320,000 Catholics were estimated by the Newman Club Federation as attending secular institutions.) Full-time students in Jesuit-conducted schools, the backbone of enrollment, were definitely on the increase, and there was an increase of 21.9% in veterans' enrollment. Soon, veterans' sons will swell the ranks. Extension courses total 2,551.

To the 25,155 students educated in the 41 Jesuit high schools of the United States, we can add 6,302 in the Jesuit high schools of the Philippines and 2,747 other Jesuit mission schools. This would bring the number of secondary school students educated during the year by American Jesuits, at home and abroad, to a total of 34,204. To the total of 97,183 collegians enrolled in the United States add also 2,753 collegians in the Philippines and 1,197 in all other mission schools. This would make an estimated total of 101,133 students in the American Jesuit Assistancy. Adding the world high-school enrollment, it makes a grand total of 134,337 secondary and collegiate-university students in the American Assistancy—an estimated increase of 9,422, or 7.5%.

Lengthy as the Society's training of its members may be, it obviously cannot take care of the specialized training needed for men who are teaching in the various departments of colleges or universities, or take up a life of special research. Any marked expansion of Jesuit institutions, or beyond them into other areas, will necessarily involve an increase in the number of laymen on the Jesuit faculties. But whether it expands or not, the Society must continue to prepare large numbers of Jesuits who by their special training will be equipped to assume responsible teaching and administrative positions in its institutions. The figures on these special studies for 1954-55 indicate that Jesuit superiors are keenly aware of such a necessity.

During the academic year 1954-55, 82 Jesuits were assigned to devote their entire time to studies beyond the normal course in the Society. Of these, 46 were studying for the doctorate, thirty for a master's or other special degrees, and six were devoting their full time to special studies without working for a degree. In addition to these 82 new students, 130 Jesuits were continuing special studies, 112 for the doctorate, twelve for a master's or other special degrees, and four for no degree.

The subject matter studied covers a wide range: anthropology, business administration, chemistry, engineering, English, geophysics, history, languages (classical and modern, including Russian and Arabic), law, mathematics, philosophy, physics, political science, psychology, social service, sociology, and the various branches of theology (ascetical, canon law, dogmatic ecclesiastical history, religion, Scripture). There was nothing parochial about the choice of institutions. In addition to those who studied in the major Catholic institutions at home and abroad, many were scattered throughout the United States and Europe, as well as Canada and Mexico. Jesuits are studying in 48 colleges and universities, 16 of them Catholic and 32 secular, located in the U.S.A. and in 19 countries of Europe, and in Canada and Mexico.

The same wide range applies to the scholarly works published by American Jesuits during 1953–54, works of original and independent research of high quality. Fields touched on were anthropology, biology, chemistry, comparative literature, education, English, history, classical languages, law, philosophy, physics, psychology, Scripture, seismology, social work, sociology, theology, and religion, for a total of 112 books, monographs, and scholarly articles.

JESUIT UNIVERSITIES, COLLEGES, AND HIGH SCHOOLS

District of Columbia

Georgetown University
Washington 7, D.C.

Gonzaga High School
Washington 1, D.C.

Alabama

Spring Hill College
Spring Hill, Ala.

Arizona

Brophy College Preparatory
Phoenix, Ariz.

California

Loyola University
Los Angeles 45, Calif.

Loyola High School
Los Angeles 6, Calif.

University of San Francisco
San Francisco 17, Calif.

St. Ignatius High School
San Francisco 17, Calif.

University of Santa Clara
Santa Clara, Calif.

Bellarmine College
Preparatory
San Jose 10, Calif.

Colorado

Regis College
Denver 4, Colo.

Regis High School
Denver 11, Colo.

Connecticut

Fairfield University
Fairfield, Conn.

Fairchild College **Preparatory**
School
Fairfield, Conn.

Florida

Jesuit High School
Tampa 1, Fla.

Illinois

Loyola University
Chicago 26, Ill.

Loyola Academy
Chicago 26, Ill.

St. Ignatius High School
Chicago 8, Ill.

Louisiana

Loyola University
New Orleans 18, **La.**

Jesuit High School
New Orleans 19, La.

St. John's High School
Shreveport 15, La.

Maine

Cheverus High School
Portland, 5, Me.

Maryland

Loyola College
Baltimore 10, Md.

Loyola High School
Towson 4, Md.

Georgetown Preparatory
School
Garrett Park, Md.

Massachusetts

Boston College
Chestnut Hill, Mass.

Boston College High School
Dorchester 25, Mass.

Holy Cross College
Worcester 10, Mass.

Cranwell Preparatory School
Lenox, Mass.

Michigan

University of Detroit
Detroit 21, Mich.

University of Detroit
High School
Detroit 21, Mich.

Missouri

St. Louis University
St. Louis 3, Mo.

St. Louis University
High School
St. Louis 10, Mo.

Rockhurst College
Kansas City 10, Mo.

Rockhurst High School
Kansas City 10, Mo.

Montana

Loyola High School
Missoula, Mont.

Nebraska

Creighton University
Omaha 2, Neb.

Creighton University
High School
Omaha 2, Neb.

New Jersey

St. Peter's College
Jersey City 6, N. J.

St. Peter's College
High School
Jersey City 2, N. J.

New York

Canisius College
Buffalo 8, N. Y.

McQuaid Jesuit High School
Rochester 6, N. Y.

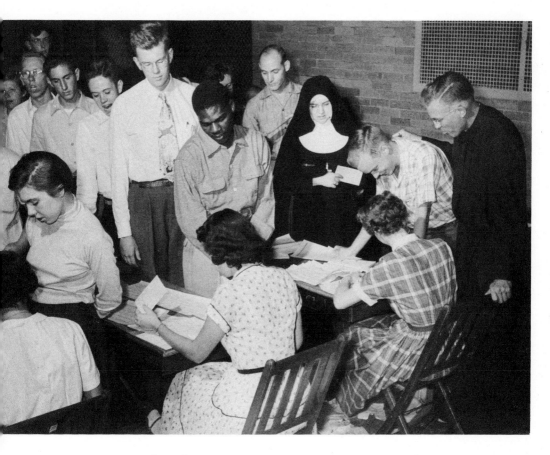

Registration day at St. Louis University.

The late Rev. Alfred J. Barrett, S. J. conducting
an outdoor poetry class on Fordham campus.

Rev. Bernard R. Hubbard, S. J. and students at the University of Santa Clara.

Rev. Raymond Feeley, S. J. and some students in his course at San Francisco University in the philosophy, dynamics, and tactics of Communism.

Le Moyne College
Syracuse, N. Y.

Fordham University
New York 58, N. Y.

Fordham Preparatory School
New York 58, N. Y.

Loyola School
New York 28, N. Y.

Regis High School
New York 28, N. Y.

Xavier High School
New York 11, N. Y.

Brooklyn Preparatory School
Brooklyn 25, N. Y.

Ohio

John Carroll University
Cleveland 18, Ohio

St. Ignatius High School
Cleveland 13, Ohio

Xavier University
Cincinnati 7, Ohio

St. Xavier High School
Cincinnati 2, Ohio

Pennsylvania

St. Joseph's College
Philadelphia 31, Pa.

St. Joseph's College
High School
Philadelphia 21, Pa.

University of Scranton
Scranton, Pa.

Scranton Preparatory School
Scranton 3, Pa.

Texas

Jesuit High School
Dallas 19, Texas

Washington

Gonzaga University
Spokane 2, Wash.

Gonzaga Preparatory School
Spokane 21, Wash.

Seattle University
Seattle 22, Wash.

Seattle Preparatory School
Seattle 2, Wash.

Bellarmine High School
Tacoma 6, Wash.

Marquette High School
Yakima, Wash.

West Virginia

Wheeling College
Wheeling, W. Va.

Wisconsin

Marquette University
Milwaukee 3, Wis.

Marquette University
High School
Milwaukee 8, Wis.

Campion Jesuit High School
Prairie du Chien, Wis.

AMERICAN JESUIT NOVITIATES
(Provinces and Vice-Province in parentheses)

Shadowbrook, Lenox, Mass. (New England)
St. Andrew-on-Hudson, Poughkeepsie, N. Y. (New York)
Bellarmine College, Plattsburg, N. Y. (New York)
Novitiate of St. Isaac Jogues, Wernersville, Pa. (Maryland)
St. Stanislaus Novitiate, Cleveland 19, Ohio
(Province of Ohio-Michigan)
Milford Novitiate, Milford, Ohio (Chicago)
Oshkosh, Wis. (Province of Wisconsin)
St. Charles College, Grand Coteau, La. (New Orleans)
St. Stanislaus Seminary, Florissant, Mo. (Missouri)
Jesuit Novitiate, Los Gatos, Calif. (California)
Sacred Heart Novitiate, Quezon City, P. I.
(Vice-Province of the Philippines)

AMERICAN TERTIANSHIPS

St. Robert's Hall, Pomfret, Conn. (New England)
Our Lady of Martyrs, Auriesville, N. Y.
(New York and Maryland)
St. Stanislaus, Cleveland 29, Ohio
(Chicago and Ohio-Michigan)
St. Joseph Hall, Decatur, Ill. (Missouri and Wisconsin)
Xavier Hall, Pass Christian, Miss. (New Orleans)
Manresa Hall, Port Townsend, Wash.
(California and Oregon)

THE THEORY OF
JESUIT EDUCATION*

THE most noticeable element in the story of American Jesuits is the growth of the schools. What is the idea behind all this educational development? The history of these schools is the story of a great adventure. Jesuit schools have left a permanent impression on four hundred years of Western civilization. Far from being outmoded, Jesuit ideas on the training of youth are very much in place at the present time.

* Many of the observations in this section are taken from an address delivered in 1940 to the Middle States Association of Colleges and Secondary Schools by the Rev. Allan P. Farrell, S.J., Dean of the Graduate School of the University of Detroit, and author of *The Jesuit Code of Liberal Education.*

The biggest problem that the Jesuits faced in inaugurating their schools was that of working out an academic program. Frequently such programs are the result of rapid action, the work of some committee that puts various bright ideas together and comes up with an attractive educational scheme. Or else they are the work of an individual genius, a born educator, a Plato, a St. Albert the Great, a Booker T. Washington, a Mark Hopkins, or a Pestalozzi. Fifteen years—1584 to 1599 —went into the preparation of the Jesuit *Ratio Studiorum,* the Latin name for what one could call in English the "Jesuit Code of Liberal Education." Into its formulation went an amazing amount of co-operation and relentless self-criticism. The core of this curriculum for undergraduates were the so-called liberal arts, and since 1599 the *Ratio Studiorum* has been the official code for Jesuit schools all over the world.

To some people the idea is strange, possibly a bit shocking, that we should be conducting schools in the middle of the twentieth century according to ideas devised nearly four hundred years ago. Certainly schools today are a very different sort of affair from what they were in 1599, and modern young people are not going to be satisfied with the curriculum of our forefathers. However, one of the most important features in educational lore is precisely the fact that certain great educational discoveries do keep their permanent value.

Ideas about the universe have greatly changed since the days of Socrates, yet his methods of teaching, by inquiry and suggestion, in informal conversation, are as much to the point today as they were twenty-five hundred years ago. Some of the accidental features of that Jesuit Code have obviously become out of date, but others remain of permanent value, some of them better appreciated at this moment than they were a generation or so past. Parents and school people alike have become dissatisfied in recent years with a type of classroom practice that completely ignores the lessons of the past, and glories in continual change. Far from vanishing off the scene, the idea of a certain degree of sane conservatism is gaining ground, and the past as well as the present is seen to have its lessons. "Real development does not mean leaving things behind, as on a road, but rather drawing life from them."

If anyone really interested in education will visit any one of the Jesuit schools today, and talk to the dean of studies or other persons in charge of the program, he will soon be convinced that the Jesuit Code or *Ratio* contains ideas and methods that are extremely pertinent to the conditions of our time.

The difficulty anyone finds who tries to write about contemporary Jesuit education is that so much in the way of principles or methods that *was* distinctively Jesuit two or three centuries ago has now passed into general practice—in public and private schools alike. It is no novelty today for a school to schedule its subject matter according to successive steps, so that the pupil will have reached one definite objective before he passes on to another. Systematic grading, and promotion according to achievement rather than by the length of time spent sitting upon a particular school bench, are now commonplace, but they were an innovation when the Jesuits began their institutions.

Particular school traditions are often easier to experience than to define; they are passed on from one generation to another more by practice than by cut-and-dried formulae. So it is with the schools of any great teaching Order, such as the Benedictines, the Dominicans, the Christian Brothers, or the Jesuits. And none can claim today a monopoly of any one educational virtue. However, if you visit a few typical American Jesuit classrooms you will notice certain features strongly emphasized.

You will immediately observe the close relationship of teacher and pupil. The Society does not wait for its men to be ordained to the priesthood before sending them out into the colleges and high schools to teach. They begin this work while they are still scholastics, that is to say, members of the Order preparing for their future priesthood. Usually they spend two or three years of teaching between their three-year seminary course in philosophy, and their four-year course in theology. This time is called the "Regency," from the old French word *régent,* used of a classroom teacher.

If I wanted to draw a characteristic picture of a Jesuit teacher, I think I would select it from this period and would show a young scholastic, perhaps with his cassock tucked up, as he spends the recess hour with his high-school boys on the playground, entering into their games, their interests and hubbub of excitement. I would follow him into the classroom, where each student is for him a personal charge, to be aided, warned, inspired, dragged mildly but firmly—even with protest—over the rough terrain that hedges Parnassus. I would look from that young teacher's desk at a roomful of—in his vision—future men: worth-while men, God-loving men, humble yet self-reliant men, charitable men, true Christian men.

Nothing that goes on in that classroom is a headline story. The AP will not teletype the news that Johnny the Goof, whose sights heretofore never rose above C's or D's, has this year, through God's wonderful grace, achieved three B's and come within striking distance of an A. *Harper's* and the *Atlantic* are not going to bid for the class genius' latest translation from the Greek Anthology. Even around the campus there won't be noise of the hot discussion that took place among the social-minded and the unsocial-minded members of the class after the visit of some Sodality members to the latest housing project on the Northeast Side.

The bond between teacher and pupil is not something you can measure statistically, or by socio-psychological measurements. It is largely a secret between the teacher, the boys, and the God who made them, though the dean may gather inklings of it as he makes his customary rounds. It is only long years later, perhaps, at some twenty-fifth reunion, that much of the hidden truth will out, and the old grad will explain what everybody knows needed no explanation: "Young Mr. Clavius (now Reverend Father Clavius, S.J.) certainly accomplished a minor miracle in getting my tongue-tied self on my feet, and making me talk connectedly and persuasively; he made me write, organize, and formulate my thoughts; and what's more, made me *think;* made me reason, put two and two together and learn why a physical experiment did prove certain scientific laws, and what you had to do to complete and to validate that proof." And Dr. Roentgen, now professor in the university medical school, wants everybody to recall how minutely Mr. Clavius insisted upon the class' preparing the passages they were studying, or the experiment they were going to perform, and how doggedly he insisted that the class repeat with new, fresh devices what they had already half-learned. "So," says the Doctor, "it would stick with us. It wouldn't all go into one of our dull ears and out the other. My present medical students growl a bit when I insist on using this worrisome Jesuit method—preparation, many-sided analysis, repetition —but they don't throw brickbats at it when examination comes around!"

Rev. Father Clavius may insert a word of his own, and ask his old pupils just how, after twenty-five years, they feel about one very sensitive and much criticized point in the typical Jesuit instruction: the stress laid upon the liberal arts, which meant not only English style, composition, and literature, but also a dose of Latin and possibly Greek as well. Was that time wasted? Was too much attention given to transmitting to the youth of today the heritage of Western culture: knowledge of authors and artists, of style, languages, habits of thought and criticism, and—most of all—certain great values, matters that you cannot neatly package into words? Should time have been allotted to material more purely technical, because we live in a technical age?

The Jesuit educator is fully aware that we need to know the skills and secrets of our various trades and professions in this highly competitive American world. But what doth it profit a man if he gain the whole world and suffer loss to his own soul? These words apply not solely to the world to come; a person needs his own soul now. In any career he needs power of judgment, reflection, choice, decision. He needs to appreciate the fine things of life: art, music, literature. If he lacks such appreciation he frustrates himself. Nothing is more woeful, for instance, than a supposedly cultivated man who is unfamiliar with even the elementary canons that govern the great productive works of the human imagination: in poetry, in the various representative arts, in music or architecture. While not everyone is gifted with an intuition that enables him to grasp the subtler workings of the creative imagination, the Jesuit believes that certain fundamental laws of beauty, proportion, and power can be taught. The old name for the freshman year in a Jesuit college was the Poetry year, as the sophomore year was called Rhetoric. But the original meaning of *poësis,* the Greek noun from which poetry takes its name, was (imaginative) *creation,* and the Jesuit believes that in every man there is some spark of that divine creative ability, and that it is the duty and privilege of the educator to elicit it.

Yet the picture is incomplete without mention of a certain profound feature of that education, profound precisely because it does not meet the eye.

If you look at the catalogue of Jesuits and the respective offices they hold, which each province prints for the benefit of its members, you will notice after the names of men who are still teaching a figure indicating the number of years they have now completed in the classroom. "Father So-and-So, *An.* 14 *mag."* is the abbreviation for *"anno 14 magister"*—that is, fourteen years a classroom teacher or "master." There are many entries which end *an. 17 mag.; an. 25 mag.; an. 39 mag.* The late Father John Brosnan, professor of physics at Woodstock College, Maryland, ran his classroom record up to sixty years of uninterrupted teaching—an amazing achievement.

These brief, cryptic figures are meager publicity, known to none but a man's fellow Jesuits. Yet they are highly prized as a record of overmastering devotion to the noblest of causes, the Christian education of the young. Moreover, they refer to something more than even the individual's record. They testify to a tremendous contribution that has been made to the cause of education as such. In the words of Father Farrell:

> The Jesuits have offered the example of 400 years of dedication to "the drudgery" of unrelieved pedagogy. There cannot but be something impressive in the spectacle of hosts of men laboring year after year to teach unnumbered thousands of ordinary people the ways of knowledge and the knowledge of God, while they themselves remained for the most part unknown, almost anonymous, and unmarked in history. There have been in these Jesuit centuries brilliant men, intellectuals and schools in every age; but no small portion of their abilities was consecrated to the toilsome trade of the teacher, many of the books they conceive written only on the minds of their pupils, and their achievements inscribed in a corporate rather than a personal record.

Let us note, too, that for these same four hundred years the Jesuits have educated not the sons of wealth, but in the main the sons of the poor, and during 300 years gave a free education to all. They accepted no fees or tuition whatsoever until forced to take a modest recompense, like all other schools in our country, in order to keep their institutions going at all. As it is, there is not a Jesuit school or college in this country which does not strain its budget to the uppermost in providing what it can of scholarships and special aid for needy students. American Jesuit educational institutions do not receive the support of the state or Government and do not expect to receive it. Their halls are built and their budgets maintained for the most part by the contributions of the poor or of people in very moderate means. Where donations or foundations have occurred, precious and important as they are, they are almost trifling in comparison with the enormous sums given or bequeathed to great secular schools. The principal factor in the final management of a Jesuit school is the merciful Providence of God. They have never yet been on easy street, and probably never will be. Today, when all private educational institutions are deeply concerned about their welfare, they make common cause with all such institutions in maintaining their integrity and their very existence.

Each of these schools represents the hopes, the determination, the generosity of hundreds and thousands of willing contributors. They are a living embodiment of a Catholic people's conviction that no educational system, however impressive, however richly endowed with talent and with apparatus, is fully true to its high calling unless it clearly and uncompromisingly places the knowledge and love of the Creator in the first place of all its activities. No individual student is obliged to attend any of these schools. Many of them could obtain easier financial accommodation, lighter study schedules, in some cases better living accommodations, by applying to other than Catholic institutions. It would have been easy for parents to shift the responsibility off to schools supported by public taxation or by wealthy foundations. In other words, it is a very easy burden to evade. But the founders and the alumni of the Jesuit schools did not see their way to evading it. They believed in the Catholic and the Jesuit idea of a school, and they were determined to see it through. And, as I have indicated, in doing so they were an inspiration to many men and women of good will in other faiths who are concerned about the condition of our secondary and higher American education; people who are willing to make certain sacrifices in order that the Creator may not be ignored in the process of learning about the wonders of His creation.

Contrary to what one might expect, the Jesuit schools for lay youth do not insist upon any overwhelming amount of formal religious teaching. Such systematic doctrinal instruction has, of course, its place and its rightful place in the Jesuit curriculum, as it had traditionally in all American schools of an earlier generation. Jesuits do not wish their pupils to play their religion by ear. They want them to know their belief's content as well as its application; to be prepared not only to live it themselves, but to be able to explain it to others. Thus in recent years American Jesuit religion teachers have been developing systematic college courses in theology. The student forms his character not only by what is taught him directly, but also by the type of world philosophy which surrounds him in his daily contacts. The basic point of view of a Jesuit school has always been professedly Christian. It reflects the belief that man was created, redeemed, and hallowed by God; that his end is God; that therefore he must learn to live in terms of God, according to God's purposes or will, if he is to achieve his destiny. "The soul of education," as a Midwestern Jesuit educator used to say, "is the education of the soul."

In applying this world philosophy to their schools, the

Jesuits never relied mainly on religious instruction, and so they did not crowd their curriculum with religious and moral subjects. Their religious attitude pervaded the schools like an atmosphere, and communicated itself directly and indirectly, by teaching contact, guidance, and example. Jesuit education has never lost sight of the basic truth that if you wish to form a man to be a Christian, you must at the same time form him to be a man. Hence its stress on a total view in liberalizing and humanizing its pupils: a policy that has a new and special significance in our own time, when even the most cautious are alarmed at the toll a technological age takes in the free expansion of the liberalized human personality.

The Jesuit college is dedicated to knowledge and to truth; it is likewise committed to the service of the community as a social institution. By its dedication to knowledge and the truth, it pursues the whole range of scientific knowledge and research; yet it is also committed to the development of the human personality. It is thus both truth-centered and student-centered. This is not contradictory but part of one integrated whole; for the development of human beings at a mature level and the basic establishment of human personality are achieved precisely through the acquisition of knowledge and truth. Under this double dedication the Jesuit college as a social institution is ordered to the service of society, both natural—the state and cultural society, and supernatural—the Church.

The objective, therefore, of the Jesuit college is to achieve the glory of God by developing human beings as such to maturity in and through a dedication to truth and intellectual culture, and thereby serving society and the Church.

Jesuit education does not rely on man's inner powers of development alone, without the grace of God. The heart of every Jesuit institution is the school or college chapel, not just a place where the requirements of religious worship are fulfilled on Sunday or other special occasions, but a spot that enshrines the very source of the school's spiritual life. The acts of worship carried out in that chapel (the principal one is the sharing in the great daily sacrifice of Holy Mass) place the student in direct relationship with the Source of all grace, the heart of the Redeemer Himself. Jesuit religion educators are now doing much to encourage student participation in the liturgy of the Mass, according to the norms laid down by the Church.

The Jesuit teacher, indeed, realizes the student's need for the grace of God since he feels so greatly his own need for it. Without grace, without himself drinking daily and ardently at the same spiritual fountain, he would lack the courage and spirit of joy needed in order to persevere under long, monotonous labor. *With* the help of that grace, the same labor becomes a precious privilege.

All this is so true that in point of fact nobody can really understand much about any person who leads a life like that of a religious-order teacher—such as a Christian Brother or a Jesuit—unless one grasps that the biggest part of such a life is precisely what is *not* seen, the life of hidden hard work, some of it known only to God. Looked at from this point of view, lives of different men in the Order do not really differ so much as they would appear. Even in the most varied and outwardly exciting career the bulk of the real effort is behind the scenes, in the toil of preparation, "home work" and research; in countless little side chores that mean nothing save to those who have been burdened with them. But some men, like these lifelong classroom teachers, belong as it were to the elite of the obscure, patient workers. The honor they hold in the Society is precisely in inverse ratio to the degree of prominence and immediate outward success with which the world rates people. They are fortunate enough to be more than ordinarily conscious of leading a life similar to that of Nazareth's divine Workman. On sure ground themselves, they can inspire a sense of sureness in those around them. Since the Society works not as a mere collection of worthy individuals but as a real *company,* a firm-knit fellowship where each one does his part for the *whole* cause of Jesus' redeeming work upon earth, the more unobtrusive outwardly are the circumstances of the individual's life, the closer is his understanding with all those who share the same experience.

And so the Jesuit who has mastered this truth—and sometimes it takes a lifetime really to penetrate its full significance —touches close to a cruelly sharp problem of our day. Where, in this crowded and ever-narrowing earth will we find the way for the tragically divided children of men to communicate with one another? How can we bridge the clefts of social, political, economic, cultural, and racial difference? How can we convey our understanding of the faith that is in us, to minds and habits a whole wide world apart? Talks at the summit may accomplish wonders, but there are also talks at the base, on the common ground of the humblest facts of our daily existence. There is an answer to this query, not so much in theory as in action. Nobody can feel wholly a foreigner when sharing the table and tools of Nazareth.

THE JESUIT BROTHER

THE preceding observations on the Jesuit teacher are all the more to the point in the case of the Jesuit brother. St. Ignatius, when he founded the Society, did not confine its membership to the company of priests who took upon themselves the Order's full responsibility and who pledged themselves with all of its promise to God. He also provided for a wide type of membership, whom he called Coadjutors. Some of these would be priests; others would not undertake to study for the priesthood, but would remain as consecrated laymen or non-priests, yet full-fledged members of the Society. These are the Coadjutor Brothers (the term

"Lay Brothers" is no longer used). As aptly put by Father James J. Daly, S.J., in his admirable little book *The Jesuit in Focus:**

> Jesuit coadjutor brothers are not mere Jesuit auxiliaries; they are Jesuits in every sense of the word. They take vows and share in all the spiritual life and spiritual privileges of the Society. They enter the Society to be brothers and to serve in the lower branches of the religious establishment, attending to its material needs and helping to create those domestic conditions which are favorable to study, prayer and the free exercise of the Society's ministry in all its various forms. . . . It would be a grave error, however, to conclude (that the brother's) lot is insignificant as well as humble. . . . The first question in the Society is, Is he a spiritual man? Not, Is he a learned man? or a competent man? or a brilliant man? Those questions may be asked; but they are not the first ones asked. And a brother can become a very spiritual man indeed. There are four brothers among the (twenty-seven) canonized saints of the Society; and among the (139) Jesuits who have been beatified, twenty-two are brothers. In evaluating these statistics it is to be remembered that the number of brothers in the Society at any time is far fewer than that of priests and scholastics. Alphonsus Rodriguez was canonized more than three hundred years after his death. He is the one confessor-saint among Jesuit brothers, that is, he was declared a saint by the Church simply because he lived the life of a Jesuit brother perfectly.

With the ideals and the living example of Jesuit brothers in mind, I wrote some years ago:†

* Milwaukee, Bruce, 1940.

† Several of the following paragraphs, as well as the first part of the chapter on "The Jesuit Apostleship" and some paragraphs relating to the coadjutor brothers under "Jesuit Activities," are taken with permission from the author's earlier book, *The Jesuit in Modern Times* (New York, America Press, 1927).

Humble labor holds the highest place of esteem in the religious life. It is not a life for dreamers and enthusiasts, but for men or women who are willing to put their hand to the plough, and work patiently, in silence and obscurity. The more humble; the more menial the form that labor takes, the more rapid a path is it to the fulfilment of a man's engagement to God. "When you work for yourselves," says Bourdaloue, "since you yourselves are small, everything is small which you do; but when you concern yourselves for God, everything that you do has in it something Divine."

The coadjutor brother's estate holds therefore a special advantage. It is not a mere plan or "economy" for the sake of securing constant and inexpensive domestic service. The position of the brother offers to men the highest privileges of the religious life, without the responsibilities of the priesthood. To the brother the life of the Order perhaps offers less to captivate the imagination than to the priest, yet the deepest and most penetrating understanding of the religious life is frequently found among the brothers, and the most intense love and loyalty to traditions and legislation of their religious family.

This practical view of the dignity of labor, though based on the concept of the supernatural mission of the Son of Man, offers nevertheless a wonderful contribution towards bridging the distance that sometimes seems to separate the priest from the layman, as well as the manual from the mental worker. In the religious life priest and layman, student and domestic toiler, are united in one common spiritual ideal, and in one common task of the service of God as rendered by the religious family. If rude labor can be honored and elevated by the goal of the religious life, how much more honor is there in that domestic co-operation, which, in the Jesuit plan, is an actual part of the priestly ministry? In the Jesuit conception, the members of the community are still more closely united by the fact that the work of those who are not priests is related to and is part of the priestly apostolate. The brother enjoys not only the dignity and merit of Christian labor: the privilege of the combined service of the whole religious family. He also takes part in the actual work of the priesthood, with which he is more intimately associated than is possible in other states of life. Spared from the priesthood's heavy responsibility, the grievous accounting for talents which must be faced by the scholar and teacher, the brother unobtrusively takes his part in the collective homage offered to God. He joins with all his other brethren in the common task of working for self-perfection. It is all one undivided endeavor for God's glory and the good of men.

The work of the brother, from the merely outward view, is one of great responsibility and practical importance. His offices are the offices of a family, not the jobs of a paid employee.

A haphazard review of some coadjutor brothers personally known, calls to mind the following occupations held by them in the writer's own Province: accountant, infirmarian, manager of printing plant, printer, assistant director of College Debt Fund, baker, cook, supervisor of Province farms, sacristan, secretary of Provincial, church decorator, tailor, porter, college infirmarian, institutional purchaser, custodian of observatory, treasurer, gardener, stenographer, steward.

The possession of knowledge or vocational training over

A Jesuit lay brother feeding chickens at Florissant, Mo.

and above the required level of common-school education **fits** the brother for the corresponding degree of responsibility.

Only those who have long been familiar with the life of a religious community can realize how far-reaching is the influence of a single devoted brother for the good and the happiness of the group as a whole. But when that work, valuable in itself, is joined to a spirit of faith, it is then lifted into the highest sphere of collective effort, and becomes the type of the lifework of the true apostle and follower of Christ.

Instead of the brother's being a sort of practical afterthought, admitted to the fellowship of others through expediency or courtesy, he is in fact the prototype of the Order man or religious. The priest-religious is a product of later evolution in the long history of religious life in the Catholic Church. During the centuries when the religious life first took definite shape, especially under the Rule of St. Benedict, the majority—in many cases practically all—of the religious were laymen. Manual toil, not the offices of the ministry, was the main occupation of the monk. Even at present the life of the Trappist and the Carthusian is largely the life of the lay worker. Those among them who happen to be priests, except for the celebration of the Mass and some few limited priestly duties interior to the monastery, live and work as non-priests. St. Francis of Assisi was not a priest, nor were the majority of his early Franciscan companions.

Owing to their solid grasp of those matters that are the common philosophy of all religious life, the brothers of the different Orders meet with one another on the closest possible ground. They form also a bond of union between the older clerical or priestly Orders and the Congregations composed entirely of lay religious which today, by their lives of tremendous fruitfulness and heroic self-sacrifice, exemplify a genuine type of the religious ideal in the Church. Since the actual life of Christ is the charter of the religious life, one cannot avoid the observation that for thirty years of that life Jesus of Nazareth lived the life of a coadjutor—the life of constant, domestic labor, and only for three years—even these abundantly mingled with humble toil—did He lead the life of the outward, priestly ministry.

Mission work, incidentally, would be hopelessly handicapped were it not for the contribution of faith, skill, and boundless resourcefulness made by the Jesuit coadjutor brothers. Of two such men as Brother Robert Benish, S.J., prefect of boys at the St. Mary's Mission, Alaska, and Brother Albert Perri, S.J., master mechanic, the veteran Alaska missionary Father Paul C. O'Connor says: "They are only two, but they are an army in themselves. Life is varied and changing for our brothers. They meet difficulties head-on. From constant contact with them for the past twenty-five years in Alaska, I have yet to find a Jesuit brother who does not graciously maneuver himself and us out of the most trying predicaments. A problem does not get them down; rather it is an occasion to prove that they have what it takes. Do you wonder why we like to have them around our mission?" The same would be the testimony of any missionary in any part of the world.

In Washington, D.C., there is an impressive clock in the tower of St. Aloysius Church at N. Capitol and Eye Streets. Few people know the story of this clock. One day in the last century a heavily built, quiet-mannered man presented himself at the Jesuit novitiate in Fredericksburg, Maryland, with the request to be accepted as a brother. He said his name was Blasius Welch.

"Have you any particular abilities or talents?" asked the master of novices as a routine requirement.

"Certainly," replied the prospective coadjutor brother. "I am an expert at washing dishes." So dishes he washed, expertly, while he grew in grace and in favor with all his companions. One day a stranger called, asking the novitiate porter if a certain Mr. Welch, who was known as a master-clock-maker, lived there. "He constructed this clock I have brought with me," said the visitor, "according to a special formula of his own, with about half the usual number of moving parts. But nobody else knows how to repair it."

"Sure, I made it," said Brother Welch, when sent for. In a very brief time he had the clock running again. "Could you make another clock like it?" asked the superior. "Certainly," said Brother Welch, "if that's what you want."

So Brother Welch got to work, and constructed a series of entirely unique clocks, built according to his special formula. One of these is in the belfry of St. Aloysius Church; others are at Woodstock College (the Jesuit higher seminary or scholasticate near Baltimore) and at the rectory of St. Ignatius Church, Baltimore (the former Loyola College). None but Brother Welch could keep the clocks repaired or regulated, save one scholastic who had mastered his secret, Mr. (later Father) Joseph M. Johnson, now of Georgetown Preparatory School, Garrett Park, Maryland.

Blasius Welch has long since gone to his reward (1897), and it was his last moments that revealed one simple but significant item in the brother's life. The "rule of silence" has its honored place in Jesuit houses as it has in the older types of monastic institutions. Certain hours, certain places in particular, are emphasized. It is not a harsh rule. The Constitutions expressly provide for all necessary exceptions, and there are plenty of chances to talk where conversation is needed for soul and body. But the rule is very pervasive and elusive. It is always so easy to imagine exceptions above and beyond those conceded. Non-silence fits naturally into our congenitally garrulous natures; it is a relief for pent-up grouches, an outlet for the quiet assertion of one's own otherwise ignored personality. For a busy person—a brother, student, or priest—it is praiseworthy to keep the rule of silence perfectly for one complete day; it is a rare feat to keep it inviolate for a week. But as he lay on his deathbed, years after his entry into the Society as an expert dishwasher, Brother Welch confided to his superior that never, in his entire Jesuit career, had he once disregarded the rule of silence.

Jesuits do not set store on prize records, on mathematical exactness and feats of asceticism. Life is too earnest and responsibility too great for the totalling up of scores of moral championship. The greatest man, in their eyes, is the humble and simple soul who acknowledges his own faults but ever strives for better. But sometimes the humility and simplicity of a man's entire life lends significance to such a record. So it was with Brother Welch; so it was too with the late Brother Vorbrinck, for almost fifty years in charge of the farm at

THE JESUIT APOSTLESHIP

IN THE mind of its Founder, the Society of Jesus was distinguished from other religious families by the fact that the entire practice of religious observances was itself directed towards the good of souls, towards the spiritual welfare of one's neighbor. The Jesuit undertakes to work for his neighbor by the practice of his own offering of religious observance. At the same time, his actual work for his neighbor offers the best opportunity for carrying out the observance itself: *Ut totum religionis pondus* (to quote the succinct words of Suarez) *illum (finem) principaliter respiciat.* "The whole weight of religious observance should bear toward the goal of the neighbor's spiritual good"—not as something added to the life of self-perfection, but as the actual essence of the observance.

In all Religious families, however, there is a difference between the broad outlines in which they are conceived by their Founder and the more distinctive traits that come as a result of their historical evolution and through the guidance of God's particular Providence in their regard. Hence the Benedictine foundations took on a variety of cultural and spiritual activities in the course of centuries, which can be considered as implied, but not expressly anticipated, in the original Rule of St. Benedict. We see, for instance, the growth of their social and agricultural mission in Germany, their liturgical development in Rome itself, their influence on civic stability in northern Italy, as well as their missionary destiny in various lands, and their educational mission in England and English-speaking countries.

The plan of Ignatius was remarkably distinct and distinctive. Yet once this apostolate was put into effect it developed certain further characteristics which were the unfolding of the original germ in the Founder's mind.

A particular activity is felt as a Jesuit work not so much by its actual nature, as by the spirit with which it is undertaken. So universal then is this scope of the Society that many of the works that are more characteristically taken up by other Orders, or by the diocesan clergy, may in some sense be engaged in by a Jesuit as circumstances demand, while still retaining the concept and spiritual motive of the Jesuit apostolate.

After making all allowances, however, one may still ask if there be not some phase of the apostolate which in point of fact, and in the main, is looked upon as characteristic of the Society of Jesus. The Benedictines, for instance, with all the latitude of their constitutions, lay stress on the solemn and worthy performance of the Church's liturgy, the *opus Dei;* the Reformed Cistercians, or Trappists, emphasize pennance combined with manual labor; the Carthusians and Carmelites lay stress on contemplation; the Friars Preachers, on the regular magistracy of preaching and teaching; the Trinitarians on the redemption of captives; the Brothers of Mercy, on corporal works of mercy; the White Fathers, on certain types of missions, and so on.

As for what concerns the ministry itself, the Society devotes itself to spiritual rather than to corporal works of charity, even though it also admits these latter, in so far as permitted by works of spiritual charity and by bodily strength. Although in its zeal the Society embraces all kinds of men, and is ready to seek the spiritual profit of all, nevertheless, in so wide a vineyard of the Lord, it exercises a certain choice of ministries and of persons to be cared for....

In its choice of ministries the Society follows this rule, that it shall seek always the greater service of God and a more universal usefulness, since the more universal a good is, the more Divine is its nature. Hence, other things being equal, it prefers ministries which confer benefit to the greatest number of men for the greatest length of time.*

* *Formula of the Institute,* Paul III and Julius III, n.1; P. VII, c.4, n.P; I, c. 3,n. 1; P. VII, c. 2, n. 1, D,D, *ad lib.*

In these words we find stated what we may look upon as the most distinguished mark of Jesuit activity. They express in somewhat more explicit form the thoughts underlying the well-known motto of the Society: *Ad majorem Dei gloriam*— "To the greater glory of God." The Society is characterized not by preference shown to any one given form of action, but rather by the choice in every direction of those works, "other things being equal," which will benefit the greatest number of men with the most solid and lasting results.

This principle may be observed as operative in the actual training given to the young men of the Society. Special aptitude and the preparation needed for particular lines of work are taken fully into consideration. Nevertheless, throughout the course of classical, philosophical, and theological studies, special care is taken to ground the candidate thoroughly for the priesthood in the principles that underlie every phase of the apostolate.

Coming then to actual works, we find that this choice of undertakings of a more universal and lasting nature results in a certain trait that may be recognized as characteristic. For want of a better word, we say that it takes on the form, in a new country like ours, of establishing the *outposts* of the Kingdom of God, rather than of administering its settled and established functions. The Jesuit appears especially in the New World as the explorer, the pioneer, or at least the pioneer settler, rather than the citizen who comes to fit into a form of life already established and past the pioneer stage.

That this should result from the idea of seeking the most universal and lasting fields of actiivty is evident enough. For the more extensive the field and the more strenuous the attempt made to implant lasting and fundamental principles, the more unusual and difficult are the conditions to be coped with.

The pioneer stage is rapidly passing from our civic life, but in the Kingdom of God these outposts will be found until the end of the world. For the spiritual *civitas,* the city of God, has to be spread by energetic labor, forethought, and personal devotion against physical and spiritual obstacles.

The metaphors under which this chivalrous concept was formerly pictured may not appeal to the modern man as vividly as they did to the romantic mind of the sixteenth century. The crusading king and the loyal knight have given place to the explorer of the air and the hero of invention and service of mankind. But the critical situation and the method that corresponds to it are entirely modern, and truer than ever at the present day.

A special situation, however, has its special requirements in the individual. He needs resoluteness and energy of character; training; mobility and readiness for movement and action; detachment from material and personal encumbrances; and, finally, a strong bond of union with the center of operations and with his fellow pioneers.

No matter how much special study may be needed for particular situations, the pioneer apostle—teacher, missionary, or preacher—needs the fundamentals of ascetic training. The practices of the noviceship are not legalistic forms. Nor are they mysterious rites calculated to lull rebellious senses to sleep and put one into a docile frame of mind. When the young man is told to break off his hour of Greek study to start peeling potatoes, or sent to wash dishes in the infirmary kitchen, it is not simply to inspire him with the fact that he is living under obedience. A training, a strengthening of mind, imagination, and will-fiber is intended; a self-mastery which in later years will not make him the hesitating victim of unexpected trifles. By mastery of petty, unreasoning impulses he is formed to carry out the great life desires of his higher, truer personality.

One thing, I think, ought to be borne in mind, that the ideal may be understood. If the qualities mentioned, such as resoluteness, energy, training, mobility, are emphasized in the Jesuit ideal, it is not from any love or emotional devotion to those qualities as such. It is that those qualities correspond to the actual situation, as its remedy. Were the situation to change, the methods and requirements would change, for they are but instruments. In private life few of us set great store by being overpunctual. Yet in an emergency exact punctuality can save a life.

The modern situation, as we see it in this country, may be summed up under four heads. Men are forgetful or ignorant of the truth. Social and economic disorder combine with physical obstacles to hinder the spread of God's Kingdom in North America. A vast world of other races and tongues lies at our doors, by whom the visible Church and her institutions are unknown or only partly understood. The Church is also faced with a supreme struggle to ensure the Christian education of youth in the United States and her dependencies. The principal phases of the Jesuit apostolate correspond to these four main phases of the American religious situation. Their single consideration affords a bird's-eye view of the field of apostolic endeavor.

Living in a predominantly non-Catholic environment, American Catholics, once they are outside the walls of their parish church, have little to remind them of their rich heritage of the Faith. A deluge of appeals to eye and ear tends from mere force of quantity to deaden the impressions of the Faith, not to speak of direct attacks on elementary morals and the foundations of religion. Hence the need of constant and careful instruction in Catholic faith and morals. Preaching and catechetical instruction are indicated, as well as the writing and publication of educative books and periodicals, suitable for every condition of life—for young and old, simple and cultivated.

With the forgetfulness of these elementary truths comes a still greater ignorance of their application to the complex problems of modern life. The interpretation, therefore, of the modern world-situation in the light of Catholic ethical and religious principles is the work of the Catholic publicist. As an outpost in the world of ideas, such an activity is peculiarly appropriate to the Jesuit plan of the apostolate. The independence from ordinary temporal considerations enjoyed by the priestly, especially by the religious publicist, as well as his training in basic principles, offers him a peculiar opportunity to cope with this especial phase of the modern situation.

The Catholic Church in the United States has been from the beginning the Church of the poor, not only in name, but in word and deed. In that title she glories, and by that title she is made like her Founder, the poor Laborer of Nazareth. Were she to cease to be the Church of the poor, were wealth, not the Faith, to determine the counsels of her leaders, it would be the beginning of the end, as it has been the downfall of the Church in times past.

Unless someone can speak for the poor man and laborer, and for the disadvantaged classes of our society, the future of the Church in the United States is doomed. If her voice were to be silent when Christian justice is violated, when discrimination and oppression are the fate of the weak, and wealth can control not only the social organism but the organs of public opinion itself, then it is but laying up anger for the day of reckoning.

But who can better speak for the poor than the man who himself is poor, and who will lose nothing he values personally were the roof burned over his head, and he were turned out to beg? Or who can better voice the condition of those elements in our Republic who suffer by race or origin, than those who have learned to prize humiliations, that they may be "clothed with the same garment and with the livery of their Lord for His love and reverence," and to suffer calumny in silence, that they may seek to imitate and follow Christ, "seeing He is the true way that leads men to life"? To speak for the poor—whether by economic want or by various forms of social discrimination—has consistently been the policy of *America,* the American Jesuits' national weekly review (founded in 1909 and published at Campion House, Jesuit House of Writers in New York City) and its companion reprint and documentary monthly *The Catholic Mind* (founded in 1904); and their editors trust this policy will never change or be found wanting.

Yet public utterance and preaching will have little effect unless there is a deepening of the character of the individual. The wonderful growth of the Laymen's Retreat movement in recent years in Canada and the United States, following the lead of many of the European countries, shows a widespread feeling that the individual's spiritual life must be deepened. The truths of the Gospel need to be brought home to him not simply as warnings or guide posts, but as the very road on which he is to travel, on which to model his thoughts, his aims, sentiments, and conduct of daily practical affairs. The *Spiritual Exercises,* which the Society of Jesus has inherited from its Founder St. Ignatius, provide this direct application of the Gospel to life: they are the program of what may be called the Catholic evangelical movement, in the true sense, without the emotionalism and unreality that term usually implies. They are bringing back the Catholic laity, men and women, to the same fountain of living waters of faith and conduct, and are a continuing source of renewed spirit for the priesthood and for religious communities.

The *Spiritual Exercises* also form the basis of the immense work of parish missions, by which the "Last Things," the great essential truths of human destiny, are unfolded not in detail to the individual in quiet reflection and personal contact, as during the Retreats, but in broad outlines preached to the masses. The parish missioner stands at the outpost against sin, vice, and ignorance. In the long hours of the confessional he touches, diagnoses, and heals with the powers given him by divine grace the intimate wounds of countless souls robbed and left bleeding on the highroad of life, and sets them on their way to their destined greatness as children of God.

Jesuit mission preaching does not mince matters in proclaiming the grim truths of sin, responsibility, eternal punishment, and the instant need of repentance. Its purpose is to stir consciences and to prepare men for a sincere return to the service of their Creator. But Jesuit preaching is never content to leave sinful human beings alone with the consciousness of their guilt. It passes from sorrow to hope; it leaves the sinner at the foot of the Cross—a triumphant Cross, enlightened with the glory of the Resurrection. Its final aim is to produce not horror but love, knowing that the supreme penitent of all ages, Mary Magdalen, won forgiveness and grace precisely because out of the grief for her sins she had conceived "much love" for the Author of all holiness. Jesuits have been criticized by moral rigorists for their insistent clinging to this note of hope, their firm confidence in the universal mercy of God. But they are convinced that this spirit, which was the spirit of their Founder Ignatius, is the spirit of the Church and of the Church's Founder, Jesus Christ. While Ignatius exhausts his imagination in depicting the evil, the cowardice, the meanness and the pestilential contagion of sin, he is equally firm in raising men from and through that consciousness to some inkling of the infinite and universal love of God for all mankind.

The movement for Laymen's Retreats is, one might say, at the other end of the mission spectrum. The retreat movement throughout the United States has grown in recent years to the point that it is now estimated that more than 250,000 men take

LAYMEN's RETREATS: The above photograph and the next in this series show Jesuit retreatants at El Retiro, California. The third photograph in this series was taken at Loyola House, Morristown, N. J.

part in at least one retreat yearly in one of the 167 retreat houses in the country. There are seventeen Jesuit retreat houses in the United States. Five of these are in the New York Province, and one of these is exclusively for priests.

This movement began in the United States on July 9, 1909, at Fordham University, where an initial retreat was given to eighteen men. Two years later, Father Terence J. Shealy, S.J., discovered a large house in Fort Wadsworth, Staten Island, which was purchased for a laymen's retreat house. On September 8, 1911, a band of fifteen retreatants inaugurated the first house of retreat for laymen in the United States. From these small beginnings the retreat movement grew throughout the United States. In the New York Province alone there were 319 Jesuit retreats and 13,280 retreatants in 1953. Jesuits also gave 500 retreats to over 30,000 retreatants in houses owned by other religious groups, and give many retreats to the clergy as well.

Each of the larger religious Orders in the Church cultivates, for historic reasons, some special devotional means for spiritualizing the life of the great masses of the Catholic people. The Carmelites promote the Scapular of the Blessed Virgin—a sort of honorary abbreviation of the habit of their Order; the Dominicans, the Rosary and the Holy Name Society; the Franciscans, the practices of the Third Order of St. Francis, the Way of the Cross, and devotion to St. Anthony of Padua; the Redemptorists, Our Lady of Perpetual Help; the Benedictines, the knowledge and appreciation of the sacred liturgy; the Augustinians, Our Lady of Good Counsel and the devotion to St. Rita. The use of these aids to a realization of supernatural truths, their spread and their preaching, is not confined to the Order with which they are traditionally identified. The religious Orders were founded in order to exert a universal influence, unrestricted by diocesan and parochial limits, though they work in co-operation and in subordination to the authorities of each diocese and parish. The Holy Name Society and the Rosary devotion are found in Redemptorist and Jesuit parishes as well as in Dominican, and so on. The interpretation of the *Spiritual Exercises* of St. Ignatius, the giving of laymen's and other retreats and parish missions is universal in the Church, and is now conducted with abundant fruit by all the Orders as well as by the diocesan clergy. So, too, with the peculiarly Jesuit devotion to the Sacred Heart of the Saviour and the spread of that devotion through the Apostleship of Prayer and through the monthly, *The Messenger of the Sacred Heart,* its chief organ of propaganda, published in New York City.

The Apostleship of Prayer is one of the world-wide spiritual societies by which the Society of Jesus reaches the laity of the world. The organization was founded in 1844 at Vals, in France, by Father Francis Xavier Gautrelet. It was first intended to cultivate an apostolic spirit in the young Jesuit students, who were there preparing for the missions. Extended by them to the villages, convents, hospitals, and other institutions in that neighborhood, in which they were teaching catechism or preaching, it soon spread throughout France and was shortly after propagated in other European countries and in the foreign missions to which these young men were sent.

Father Gautrelet's foundation was organized and perfected

by Father Henri Ramière, S.J., whose admirable work on the Apostleship of Prayer, a development of Father Gautrelet's books under the same title, gave the Apostleship new life and vigor, while *The Messenger of the Sacred Heart,* which he also founded as a monthly organ of the Association, was soon reproduced in several languages and circulated throughout the world. At present there are local centers the whole world over, with a membership estimated at forty million; of these, nearly six million have been registered as Associates of almost fifteen thousand centers established in the United States.

The goal of the Apostleship is the salvation of souls. The means by which the members of the Apostleship are to achieve that goal is through devotion to the Sacred Heart. Before the time of St. Margaret Mary, men loved and honored the Heart of Christ. But in His revelations to her, Our Lord indicated that this devotion was really a special instrument by which the graces of salvation were to be won for others. Because it is apostolic in purpose, and because the principal means used is prayer, the organization is therefore called the Apostleship of Prayer, and it has promoted First Friday practices, especially Holy Hours and Communions of Reparation.

Devotion to the Sacred Heart and the spread of that devotion are now universal in the Church, are not confined to Jesuit activity. Apart, however, from the formal recognition given by the Holy See, through special indulgences and other privileges, each Order is conscious of a certain appropriateness and ownership in the case of that particular means of spiritualization which happened, in God's Providence, to be confided to its members, and which in some way is bound up with its own history.

There is an inner tradition, a warmth of sentiment, an intimate connection with the whole structure of daily observance, felt in the case of the traditional devotional and spiritual practices of each Order. This is amply illustrated in the case of the Dominicans and Franciscans. So, too, for the Jesuit the book of the *Spiritual Exercises* is bound up with the history, the Constitutions, and the rules of his religious family, with its personal traditions and the entire tradition of its apostolic endeavor, in a way that makes the interpretation or preaching of that book felt as specially his own, while at the same time its use is thrown open to all who can find help therein.

It is a striking fact that practically the first institutions established by St. Ignatius were not primarily educational, nor religious, nor for the purpose of immediate charitable relief, but with a distinct *social* end in view. By establishing homes where, under the care of educated and pious women, wayward girls might be brought back to an honorable place in society, Ignatius showed himself a pioneer in modern social welfare endeavor. The tradition of interest in social works and a social outlook has always been a characteristic of the Jesuit ministry.

Rev. Richard J. Scannell, S. J. has been chaplain of Alcatraz Federal Penitentiary (shown in background) for twenty years.

Rev. Bernard R. Hubbard, S. J., the well-known "Glacier Priest."

Rev. Francis J. Heyden, S. J., expert on eclipses and member of the faculty of Georgetown University.

Rev. Alphonse M. Schwitalla, S. J., Dean Emeritus, Saint Louis University School of Medicine.

Rev. Francis A. DiBenedetto, S. J., Professor of Physics at Loyola University, New Orleans.

The late Rev. William D. O'Leary, S. J., director of radio station WWL, New Orleans, is shown with members of the "Dawnbusters" program.

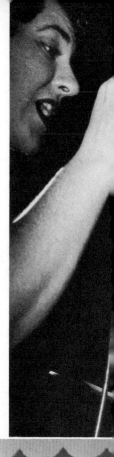

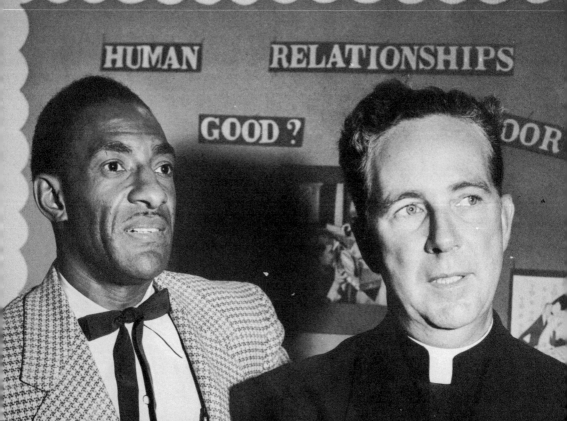

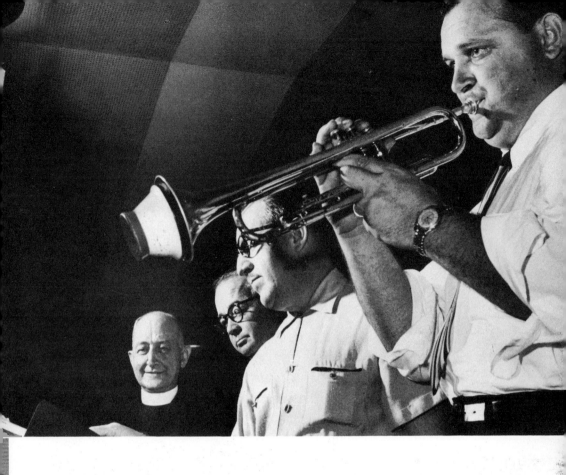

Rev. George H. Dunne, S. J. and Mr. Alton Thomas, execu-
tive secretary of the Urban League of Phoenix, Arizona.

Father Dunne and Mr. Thomas visiting the students of
Phoenix Union High School during their recreational period.

JESUIT ACTIVITIES

AT THE conclusion of his training, the Jesuit priest may be designated for any one of a very wide variety of posts and occupations, as wide a variety perhaps as one would find in any organization of its size whose members are subject to one common head. By the time he has neared the end of his course, a Jesuit as a rule has a fairly good idea of the type of work that personally awaits him, especially where such work has required some special preparation. The Order, in fact, encourages a young man to express any reasonable preferences, and expects him to make fully known to his superiors any special talents he may possess. Nevertheless, the Society still retains its entire freedom to place a man or to remove him from office as the greater good of God's work and of the Church whom the Society serves shall appear to require. The individual knows, from his own experience, from the Society's laws and its traditions, that such choices will be made with the utmost care; as far as can humanly be prevented they will not be arbitrary or fanciful. But his absolute trust rests upon no such considerations, however worthy they may be. His faith and his hope are in God our Lord, who works through human interests and arrangements. Whether that which is handed to him seems reasonable or not, he is strong always in one certainty. As long as he on his part lives faithfully up to his vocation as a Jesuit, his assignment will be the means for the working out of God's will, for his own good and for that of countless others.

The schools themselves cover an ample choice of positions with their various departments and their extracurricular activities. Four of them—Boston College, Canisius College (Buffalo), Fordham University, and Loyola College (Baltimore)—conduct schools of adult education. Departments dealing with business, commerce, and finance form part of sixteen Jesuit colleges and universities. Dentistry is taught in seventeen, education in four, general engineering in six—Spokane, Loyola (Los Angeles), Milwaukee, Seattle, Detroit, and Santa Clara, (California), while St. Louis University conducts special engineering departments in Aeronautical Technology and Geophysical and Industrial Technology.

Fifteen colleges and universities, including St. Louis University, conduct labor schools, some of them entitled "Institutes of Industrial Relations." St. Louis University features

Anno), and has since received the approbation of Pius XII.

As the General in Rome had forecast, the summer of 1934 brought the first great strike on the San Francisco waterfront and led to the bloody rioting that favored the rising star of Harry Bridges. Writers in the Jesuit national weekly, *America,* such as Fathers Richard A. Tierney, Paul L. Blakely, Joseph Husslein, and Wilfrid Parsons, had sounded and continued to sound a warning note. The present author also drew attention to the urgent need for a positive as well as a negative anti-Communist program in his writings and lectures. Thus, under pressure from Rome to "do something" and aware of the social upheaval the Depression was causing, the Jesuits insisted upon the critical importance of the working man, who very soon could be at the top. As Father William J. Smith, S.J., wrote in 1941: "The working class is climbing into the saddle. It may not be long before the reins of government are in their hands. . . . Theoretically, the Church has never failed to supply the principles for a sound labor movement. In practice, however, we have been woefully late in bringing the social doctrines of Christ down to the level and into the midst of the workers."

In 1935 the American Jesuits and other Catholic clergy held their first conference on the problem; other Catholic labor work, such as the organization of ACTU (Association of Catholic Trade Unionists), did not come until 1937. Father Raymond T. Feely of San Francisco, however, started his investigation of the San Francisco waterfront situation right after the 1934 strike. Finally, representatives of every Jesuit institution on the East Coast met in Philadelphia to decide on a course of action. At this meeting they decided to start informal adult schools to teach the workingman a philosophy of social action. The courses would be practical, not theoretical.

Just two weeks after the conference, Father Richard M. McKeon started the first Jesuit labor school in Philadelphia. Soon afterward, schools were begun in Manhattan and Brooklyn, followed more slowly by schools further west. Offering courses in parliamentary procedure, public speaking, arbitration, negotiation, and anything else a union man needs to know, the Jesuits also taught their students how to oust Communists whenever these were in control of the union. It was not until 1937 that the schools shaped into the final form of labor-management schools they are today. Now almost a third of the ten thousand students who take the eight- to ten-week courses in one of the seventeen Jesuit schools across the country are management men.

Usually management men and workers start studying in separate classes, but very often the Fathers are able to get them together to study the same subjects and discuss in the class their varying points of view. Almost from the beginning the Jesuits who have started the Institutes of Industrial Relations have found themselves carried beyond the classroom into the push and pull of the labor man's struggle. Father John M. Corridan, the famous "waterfront priest" of New York, by working with small groups of men, by keeping confidential his contacts within the International Longshoremen's Association and even the city police, has developed a behind-the-scenes power and knowledge which no one else can duplicate. Father Dennis Comey has become official arbitrator on the Philadelphia waterfront, and a number of the priests have served as unofficial arbitrators in a number of industries. Father Leo C. Brown, of St. Louis University (Institute of

Father Denis Comey talking to Philadelphia longshoremen and descending into ship's hold to inspect controversial cargo.

Social Sciences) has been kept continually active for several years to the very limit of his physical capacities by complicated and far-reaching arbitration cases submitted to his expert judgment.

In the words of Father William J. Smith, who heads an Institute at St. Peter's College, Jersey City: ·

> Only by eliminating the abuses of the capitalistic system can we keep submerged the threat of Communism. Look at the U.S. industries with Communistic or racketeer-controlled unions and in nearly every case you find a management that deserved such a union because they thwarted labor's natural growth until a powerful and embittered organization forced itself among them.
>
> We want to instill a sound social philosophy in our men. We aren't giving them a Sunday-school line. We want to show the men what they have the right to demand management to consider, but at the same time we want the union to recognize its obligation to consider the competitive situation. Ideal solutions aren't always possible.

Similar views are voiced by Father Benjamin L. Masse, industrial-relations editor of *America,* by Father John Friedl of Kansas City, Missouri, and by Father Joseph P. Fitzpatrick, of Fordham University, though with varying degrees of emphasis. One of Father Masse's outstanding achievements was that of convincing the Congress of Industrial Organization (CIO), under the presidency of the late Philip Murray, of the need for a positive and effective repudiation of the Communists who had attempted to gain the organization's higher control. He is likewise deeply convinced that the surest path to industrial peace lies not in a wishful-thinking attempt to abolish all tensions between labor and management, but rather in a constant

growth by all parties concerned in mutual respect and understanding of the others' real difficulties and real problems.

The world of apostolic activity that opens up to the young
Jesuit may not be a school world at all, but that of one or the
other of the many parishes that Jesuits conduct in various
large cities throughout the country, besides the rural parishes
in our home missions. Or he may be attached to a Jesuit radio
station, to broadcast Christ's teachings through the airwaves.
At the time of writing, Father J. Edward Coffey, an American
Jesuit from Bayonne, New Jersey, directs the English-language
short-wave broadcast on the Vatican radio station in Rome.

The following radio stations are conducted by Jesuits of
the American Assistancy: Fordham University (WFUV), education; Georgetown University, campus; Holy Cross College,
campus; St. Louis (WEW), commercial, and also TV, co-operative and commercial; University of Detroit, TV, educational and co-operative; Boston College, co-operative network,
educational; Loyola University of the South (WLW), commercial; Marquette University (Milwaukee); Gonzaga University (Spokane); and the University of Scranton.

Special to the Society is the continent-wide Sacred Heart
radio program, with headquarters in St. Louis, but relayed
through various regional offices around the country and, in
Spanish, for Latin America. Every day for the past sixteen
years, the "Voice of the Apostleship of Prayer" has been on the
air. This in itself is something of a record in the annals of
radio. In an amazing total of over 1,250,000 broadcasts, the
Sacred Heart Program has carried the message of Christ's love
over five continents, in three languages—English, Spanish, and
French. Steadily the number of outlets has grown in the

United States, Canada, Vatican City, Malta, the Philippines, Australia, India, Central and South America, Labrador, Greenland, and Formosa, until now the goal of more than a thousand stations has finally been reached.

It is a saga of wonderful co-operation, zeal, sacrifice, planning, and the Providence of God. All the radio time is donated by stations—millions of dollars' worth. Nearly all the work is done by volunteers—hundreds of them. Costs are ridiculously low compared to the "big budget broadcasts," both religious and secular.

What have been the results of this vast radio apostolate? Over a million and a half pictures of the Sacred Heart have been distributed free to listeners. An estimated million families and homes have been consecrated to the Sacred Heart. Ten thousand inquirers have been enrolled in the Home Study Course in Religion, with a great number of resulting conversions. Thousands of sick and shut-in invalids have been banded together in a union of sacrifice, zeal, and suffering for the missions and for the Holy Father. Hundreds of thousands have enrolled in the Apostleship of Prayer.

All through the years, the format of the program has remained the same: fifteen minutes of prayer reverently said, hymns beautifully sung, and short informative talks by expert radio speakers. Music is furnished by the best choirs and artists in America and Europe.

Father Eugene P. Murphy, S.J., director of the program, and the man chiefly responsible for its development, initiated a television version of the Sacred Heart Program this year. It uses the same format as the radio broadcast and will be distributed on films to stations in the United States and abroad.

On a very different level, the work of the Catholic Evidence Guild enlists the activity of educated laymen in bringing the message of the Church directly to the man on the street corner. Founded by the late Father Francis P. LeBuffe, S.J., author of a highly popular series of thoughtful devotional and apologetic books and pamphlets, it is now directed by Father Eugene K. Culhane, S.J. Father LeBuffe in the East, co-operating with Father Daniel Lord and his associates in the Mid-West, was particularly active and resourceful in restoring to some of its pristine vigor the Society's ancient and cherished Roman-form institution for apostolic lay action, the Sodality of the Blessed Virgin.

If the Jesuit is called to the relative seclusion of the laboratory, the research library, or the experiment station, the examples of many eminent men, living and dead, will be there to inspire him. Jesuits in this country and abroad have won considerable prominence in the field of astronomy and in physical science, particularly in the field of geophysics and in seismology, the recording and analysis of earth movements or earthquakes. Leadership in this field has been greatly facilitated by a chain of Jesuit seismological observatories that extends around the world, including in the United States such widely separated spots as Weston (Massachusetts); New York City; New Orleans; St. Louis, and Santa Clara (California). Dean of the Jesuit geophysicists was Father James B. Macelwane, of St. Louis University, a former president of the Seismological Society of America and recipient, in 1948, of the Bowie Medal of the American Geophysical Union. Father Macelwane, recently deceased, was chairman of the Technical Panel on Seismology and Gravity of the United States National

Committee for the International Geophysical Year (IGY),
1955-1956.

The name of Father Bernard R. Hubbard, the "Glacier
Priest," professor of vulcanology and geophysics at the University of Santa Clara, is known to millions through his brilliant lectures and writings. Father J. Joseph Lynch, director
of Fordham's geophysical observatory; Father William Re-
petti, of Georgetown, former director of Manila's seismological observatory; and Father Daniel Linehan, of Weston, are
among those who keep the public alive to the meaning of the
incessant tremors of our unquiet globe. Father Francis J. Heyden, now teaching and doing research at Georgetown, was
astronomer of Manila Observatory from 1932 to 1934, and a
member of several national eclipse expeditions.

In this country at the date of writing are Father Walter J.
Miller, research specialist in astronomical spectroscopy and
assistant director of the Vatican Observatory in Rome, and
Father Charles Deppermann, former director of the Manila
Observatory, investigating the vast and complex area of meteor-
ology, which looks after the paths and areas of destructive
storms in the Pacific area. National known figures, too, in the
field of scientific research and teaching are Father Alphonse
Schwitalla, for many years president of the National Catholic
Hospital Association; the biologist, Father Patrick F. Yancey,
of Spring Hill College, Alabama, a member of the board of
the National Science Foundation; Father Charles Berger, of
Fordham University, the only Catholic in the National
Academy of Sciences; and Father John Mullaly, working on
algology at Loyola University of the South, New Orleans.

World-wide interest is shown today in everything relating
to primitive man, past or present, and many of the most in-

teresting contributions of the Society lie in the field of anthropology. Long before anthropology was known as a distinct science, pioneering scientific work was performed by Jesuits both of the old and of the restored Society. As early as 1724, Father Joseph Lafitau, S.J., then engaged in mission work in Canada, interpreted correctly, as implements of ancient man of the Stone Age, paleolithic implements that were unearthed at that time in France. He offered this interpretation on the basis of his experience of the same types of instruments among his Indian converts. In Vienna, in 1784, Father Martin Dobrizhofer, S.J., published his studies of the Indians of South America. The Jesuit Relations, or missionary records, both French and Spanish, were mines of information concerning the ethnology, botany, geography, history, and languages of the Western Hemisphere, and Father Andrew White included some of these in his reports on Maryland.

Jesuit scholars were not slow to realize the value of the information contained in their missionaries' reports, and commented upon them, as tests of their own moral and theological principles. That very readiness is the best refutation of the oft-repeated but unsubstantiated charge that the Jesuits of the sixteenth and seventeenth centuries were mere parrots, passing on the stereotyped theses of decadent scholasticism. Men like the French Jesuit, Gaston Laurent Coeurdoux, and the Spaniard, Lorenzo Hervas y Panduro, anticipated conclusions generally accepted later in the field of comparative languages, while others wrote extensive compositions in the difficult languages of India and China, and the Indian tongues of North, Central, and South America.

In the field of paleontology, the recent epoch-making discoveries in Shensi and Kansu, China, of the French Jesuit,

Father Pierre Teilhard de Chardin, were cut short by his death in New York City in April, 1955. He had found conclusive evidence that the Sinanthropus of Choukoutien, first unearthed in 1929, was certainly human. In recent years Father J. Franklin Ewing of Fordham University and Father Joseph Doherty of the New England Province succeeded in unearthing the skeletal remains of a youth at Ksar-'Akil in Lebanon, with an estimated antiquity of sixty thousand years. American Jesuit missionaries and mineralogists are now in correspondence with paleontological experts all over the world.

The Jesuit's call may be to literary or editorial work: to become an apostle of the press, following in the long line of Jesuit authors, or in the editorial offices of one of the many Jesuit publications to carry the word of God across this world. These may be loosely classified as follows:

Magazines of general interest: *America* and *The Catholic Mind,* already mentioned; *Thought,* a critical and intellectual quarterly published under the auspices of Fordham University; the *Messenger of the Sacred Heart* and *Jesuit Missions,* with respective editorial offices also in New York City; *The Queen's Work,* monthly organ of the Sodality of the Blessed Virgin Mary, published in St. Louis; *Social Order,* a monthly specializing in the analysis and constructive treatment of crucial social problems, published by the Institute of Social Science, St. Louis; *Review for Religious,* St. Mary's College, Kansas; *Philippine Studies* (Manila), a general quarterly.

Magazines devoted to special disciplines: *The Jesuit Educational Quarterly,* New York City; *Fordham Law Review,* *Georgetown Law Review, Marquette Law Review,* and *Uni-*

versity of Detroit Law Journal; The Historical Bulletin, St. Louis University; *The Classical Bulletin, The Modern Schoolman,* St. Louis University, philosophy; *The Jesuit Science Bulletin,* Boston College; *Wasmann Journal of Biology,* University of San Francisco; *Theological Studies,* a quarterly, Woodstock College, Maryland; *Theology Digest,* St. Mary's College, Kansas; *Mid-America,* historical studies, St. Louis University; *The Woodstock Letters,* Jesuit historical and biographical records, for private circulation only. These lists do not include the many localized mission publications.

The Jesuit's call may be to the various specialized works of charity, such as the work for the blind and for the deaf in New York City or special groups, such as the Spanish-speaking in the Northeast and Southwest. Or to the hospitals, where souls in pain need the comfort of Christ, and deep insight into human nature and understanding of God's will is necessary to console and strengthen those who suffer; where numberless souls, detached from ordinary earthly occupations, clamor for instruction in Christ's doctrine.

Besides lifelong consecration to the lonely and self-sacrificing service of the hospitals and prisons, and especial care of the blind and the deaf, the American Jesuits are devoted to the spiritual help of the mentally ill. There are always certain members of the Order whose entire life is given to the task of bringing hope and order into the confusion and despair of those who are beyond the reach even of the most skilled psychiatrist.

Many Jesuits serve as chaplains of prisons, including the famous Alcatraz prison in San Francisco Harbor.

If he volunteers, as many Jesuit priests do, to serve as a

chaplain in any one of the Armed Forces, he may be chosen for this honorable work by the ecclesiastical authorities and by his own superiors. At present ninety-two American Jesuits are in the chaplain service (Organized Reserve Corps, active duty, Army and Air Force; National Guard; U. S. Navy Reserve; Auxiliary Chaplains; Civilian Air Patrol; Veterans Administration hospitals).

One Jesuit activity of a quite unfamiliar type is that of the Russian Center, attached to Fordham University in New York City. The little community of Soloviev Hall (as their residence is called), have adopted the Eastern (Byzantine) rite, with the purpose of co-ordinating Catholic religious work among the Russians in this country and preparing themselves for work in Russia itself, if that country's barriers to entrance are ever removed. The residence, with its little Byzantine chapel, is a center of information concerning Russian religious affairs. The Russian Center publishes books, leaflets, and ikons (Eastern-style religious pictures). Today there are seven Jesuit priests in the United States and two brothers in the Russian Byzantine rite. They usually follow the Russian custom of wearing beards, but beards are not required. Of the seven priests, one was born in the United States, four were born in England, and two in Russia. One of the brothers was born in the United States, the other in Czechoslovakia.

Rev. John Ryder, S.J. celebrating Mass in the Byzantine rite.

The Holy Eucharist shown under the species of both bread and wine.

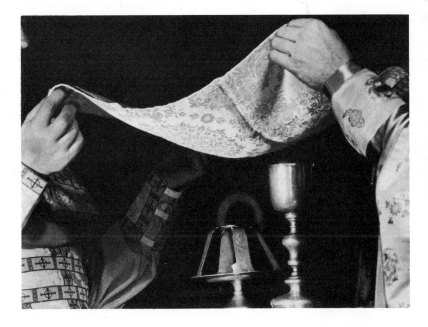

The chanting of the Gospel, and (below) members of the congregation coming forward to kiss the cross. Father Ryder is shown on next page behind iconostasis or image screen.

AMERICAN JESUIT MISSIONS

SOME of the most striking photographs in this collection are from the American Jesuit missions, taken mostly in the difficult tropical mission of British Honduras and Honduras in Central America, under the care of forty-nine Jesuits of the Missouri Province. Less than a hundred years ago, on the eve of our Civil War, Jesuits in the territory of the present United States numbered few more than seven hundred and, of these, approximately one-third were missionaries from Europe.

The beginning of the twentieth century found in existence

only two Jesuit provinces in the United States, Maryland-New York and Missouri. Even then, a mere fifty years ago, the total number of Jesuits of American birth was not as great as the number now serving in the mission field. Jesuits from the Province of Turin labored on the California Mission, whose territory included the great Northwest. Jesuits from the Province of Germany served in the region of the Great Lakes as members of the Buffalo Mission.

The emergence of America, within our own lifetime, from a mission territory into a stronghold of the Faith has kept pace with her development as a world power. Europe, the great nursery of valiant missionaries in the past, has seen the depletion of her missionary resources, ravaged by two world wars and Communism's subsequent aggressions. It is the judgment of the Holy Father himself, echoed repeatedly by apostolic delegates and bishops in mission lands, that the future of the missions lies, in great measure, in the hands of the Church in America—the bishops, the clergy, the religious Orders and brotherhoods, the sisterhoods and the laity. The response to the appeal for mission vocations has been typical of American generosity. For in the single decade from 1940 to 1950, American priests, brothers, and nuns more than doubled their numbers in the foreign missions and will soon reach the five thousand mark. Of the six thousand Jesuits engaged in mission work around the globe, 1,129 are Americans, in charge of 16 missions, speaking 24 languages, caring for 1,208 mission centers over a total area of some two million square miles.

These bald figures may seem more intelligible if we break them down into the countries served. Each Jesuit Province takes care of a particular mission or group of missions, and only by exception (or "loan") are men taken for a particular mission from outside the Province to which it is assigned.

IN ASIA

The Philippines, with 468 men, including an archbishop and a bishop, are served by the largest group of Jesuits in any single mission in the world. New York Jesuits at the request of the Holy See replaced the Spanish Jesuits there in 1921. Their mission work in Luzón and Mindanao is very diversified. Chiefly in Mindanao they operate 27 mission centers with 261 outstations. Educational work, however, is much more extensive. Their colleges (known as *Ateneo's*) are well known throughout the Islands from Manila to Zamboanga. There are eight of them, including the famous university, the Ateneo de Manila, and one that is swiftly approaching it in prominence, the Ateneo de Cagayan. In addition to their colleges they conduct or direct 19 high schools. Students from these schools do most of the teaching in 77 catechetical centers throughout the Islands. The training of Filipino priests, so important to the Church, is accomplished by the Jesuits in four large seminaries. Among their other works are the training of labor leaders, an agricultural school, the care of lepers and retreat work.

Ceylon (Province of New Orleans): 52 men.

China and Formosa (Province of California): 52 men, of whom only seven are now left in China itself—five in a Communist jail, two others under house arrest. The rest are ministering to the local Chinese and the Chinese in exile in the Philippines and elsewhere.

Jamshedpur (Province of Maryland): 53 men. A center of India's steel industry, where one of the major tasks is educating for labor leadership along Christian lines.

Patna in India (Province of Chicago): 165 men. The missionaries from this large and extremely active territory accepted recently the invitation of the Government of the Province of Nepal, hitherto inaccessible for the outside world, to establish a school at Nepal's capital, Katmandu.

Japan: 28 men. Here American Jesuits associate as part of four hundred of their Order from various countries, in a work where higher education—at the universities of Tokyo (Sophia University) and at Naga—plays a capital part.

Korea. Under particularly favorable auspices, American Jesuits from the Wisconsin Vice-Province will open a university at Seoul, in this grievously war-torn country, in the fall of 1957.

IN THE MIDDLE EAST

Baghdad College, in the Kingdom of Iraq, has brought the talents of fifty New England Jesuit educators to the land that was credited—in the past—with being the cradle of the human race, and—in the present and the indefinite future—is known as the hottest place in summer where any human being attempts to live on this globe. But the College of Baghdad has become an important part of the nation's life.

IN THE SOUTH PACIFIC

This New York Jesuit mission of the Caroline and Marshall Islands, which cares for a brave, seafaring people scattered over two million square miles of ocean, has just suffered a severe loss in the death on September 29, 1955, of its bishop, the Most Reverend Thomas J. Feeney, S.J. The Bishop's motto, *Laetentur Insulae Multae* ("Let many islands rejoice"), is being literally fulfilled, as a result of his own and his thirty-eight companions' efforts.

IN THE AMERICAS

The Province of Oregon looks after the missions of Alaska, which the late Pope Pius XI referred to as the most difficult missions on earth. The late Father Francis Barnum, S.J., one of the territory's pioneer apostles, used to tell us that when an Alaska missionary finally made his way through snow and Arctic gales to the mission center, nobody expected him either to greet or to be greeted. He simply lay on the floor of the mission residence until he had recovered enough energy to talk. The story, whether correct or not, is symbolic of the hardships which the forty-two men of this, one of the oldest of the present-day American Jesuit missions, have to endure.

Paths to the remote corners of the Honduras missions are in some cases through the vast, dense tropical jungle; in other instances, across the plains or along its numberless water courses and stretches of ocean front; in all of which journeying the sail and the mule still play an important part. But still more important in this mission, as in the other Caribbean territory of Jamaica, is the part played by the development of co-operatives and credit unions in enabling the farmers, ranchers, and fishermen to help their own livelihood. In every country where they must cope with problems of poverty and destitution, American Jesuits are convinced of the fact—which took some time and persuasion to be accepted by many conservative minds—that education in sound co-operative methods is one of the most important ways to enable people to live as men and not as beasts, to keep the integrity of the individual family, and to prepare its members for Christian citizenship.

In the lovely island of Jamaica, in charge of seventy-nine Fathers of the New England Province, 85,000 Catholics may seem a small number in comparison with a total population of 1,420,000. But the influence they wield in the entire Jamaica community compensates for their small number. Much of their influence is to be attributed to the fact that the Jamaica mission from the beginning has stood for higher education.

Here at home, forty-five Jesuits are devoted to the work for the American Indians in the states of Idaho, Montana, Wyoming, South Dakota, Washington, Utah, and Michigan. Their mention calls up the memory of such mighty pioneers as Father Peter de Smet, in the Plains country, Father Cataldo, in the Northwest and other men—priests and coadjutor brothers—who won the Indians' esteem and friendship at a time when most white men persecuted them and robbed them of their lands.

Jesuits from the days of the early Maryland missions have worked among the Negroes in this country; today some thirty-eight Jesuits are assigned to Negro mission work, mostly in Maryland and Louisiana, although some are in the large cities; while forty-five are engaged in home mission work with the Spanish-Americans. Ascribed to the various missions, but temporarily absent from them either because of special studies or ill health, are, at this writing, 163 priests and scholastics.

To form any fair picture of what all this means, one needs to keep in mind two or three great aspects of the world mission field.

First of all, the ruling trait of Jesuit mission work abroad remains the same as that which it so characteristically features at home: its strong emphasis upon education—education at all levels, and notably upon higher education, at the college and university, and even the graduate, level.

In the American Jesuit missions, members of the Society conduct fifteen universities and colleges, besides the university soon to be opened in Seoul, Korea. They likewise staff 23 high schools and six seminaries for the native clergy. In addition to this, they direct 66 high schools, 280 elementary schools and 71 medical dispensaries. All this in addition to serving 198 mission churches, 24 hospitals and 26 orphanages.

Their mission work ranges from the humblest apostolate of the bush, jungle, and beach, as among the Santals of India, the Eskimos of Bering Straits (in sight of Soviet Siberian outposts), the mountain paths of Jamaica, the seafarers and fisherfolk of the South Pacific all the way to the libraries, laboratories, and lecture halls of Baghdad, Katmandu, Batticoloa, or Tokyo.

Except for the change of climate, of language, of complexion, and perhaps hours of daily schedule, the Jesuit who has taught second-year high in New Orleans, Boston, Milwaukee, or any other of our large cities finds no tremendous change when he faces his bunch of young hopefuls in Trincomalee, Cagayan, Belize, or Jamshedpur. No other American organization, Protestant or Catholic, has a greater world stake in foreign education than have the American Jesuits.

At the same time, recent years have seen enormous changes in the conditions under which the missions operate, changes which in their turn greatly tend to lessen the gap between country and country, between educational and pastoral work at home and the work in the mission field. Distances have shrunk to a heretofore incredible degree. We contrast with present-day world airline transportation not only the year it took for St. Francis Xavier to get from Portugal to the shores of the East Indies, but even the several weeks of combined land and sea travel that burdened missionaries and mission superiors a generation or so ago. But great as are the physical changes, social and political conditions have shifted the scenes to an incredible degree for the missionary. As a white man (with a few exceptions) and the representative of a white man's culture and of a religion that in the mission-sending countries is largely administered by white men, he offers his services today to the people of nations which, for the most part, have rid themselves once and for all of the colonial political tutelage.

Moreover, the people of these "mission countries" are today, for the most part, acutely conscious of the enormous economic disparity between the mission-sending countries—European or American—of the Atlantic or temperate zones, and their own near or actual destitution. Said an old Scotch sea captain to me one day as he apologized for taking my time after the late Mass on a hot Sunday in southern Maryland: "It's ill talk, they say, between a fu' man and a fastin'." Lest any such "ill talk" arise, today's missionary needs to be a sign of hope to his people in their humble temporal problems, something that is in no way alien to his preaching to them the message of eternal life. After all, did not our blessed Lord Himself feed that five thousand in the wilderness? Today's missionary cannot, as a rule, expect to work economic miracles, but he can, and most effectively does, accomplish a lot toward making it easier for the families under his care not only to believe in the Christian Faith, but also to practice it in their homes. The need of such truly fatherly care is particularly evident when the missionary comes from a country that controls so much of the world's wealth and political power as does the United States. Our country's accumulated store of technical know-how is a god-send to these same peoples. Our American missionaries, Jesuit and non-Jesuit alike, are generously imparting to them an understanding of co-operative and agricultural techniques as they have been elaborated in this country and Canada. In many cases the American missionary can achieve far-reaching results by an intelligent use of the facilities provided by the various agencies of the United Nations and UNESCO, as well as by the technical aid programs of our own Government.

As the vast masses of the various non-white peoples of the world grow in their sense of native national consciousness, the importance of a native clergy becomes increasingly evident. American Jesuits do not forget that it was a former Jesuit of the old eighteenth-century English Maryland mission, Father John Carroll, chosen by his fellow priests for the Holy See's appointment as the first Catholic bishop in the newly organized Republic, who stood out firmly for a native American clergy and an American seminary (St. Mary's, Baltimore), at a period when the United States, as a mission land, was largely evangelized in the Catholic Faith from Europe. Following Bishop (later Archbishop) Carroll's tradition, the Society in our time has set itself squarely for the training of vocations from the different mission lands where it operates, beginning with the Jamaica and the Philippine missions, and continuing the same policy elsewhere. In the Jesuit diocese of Kingston, Jamaica, the chancellor, the Rt. Rev. Monsignor Gladstone O. Wilson, is a native Jamaican. This enlightened policy is particularly fruitful in the Philippines, where of the two Jesuit members of the Philippine Hierarchy—Archbishop James T. G. Hayes and Bishop Aloysius del Rosario—the latter is a native Filipino.

"American Jesuits," at present, include an ever-growing proportion of members of the Society—scholastics, priests, and brothers—who themselves are natives of the various mission lands, the furthest advanced in this respect being the Philippines, where a considerable proportion of the members of the American Jesuit mission are themselves Filipinos, along with some members of Chinese or Japanese origin. When such a development has reached its full maturity, the mission itself ceases to be a "mission" any longer. Like the Church here at home, it becomes a part of the fully organized Church in that country, in its own right.

At this point someone who reads this story in one of the aforesaid mission lands—and many a mission-minded person in the United States—is pretty likely to ask: How about our attitude to persons of other races in the United States itself? For our conduct in that respect is sharply scrutinized by the converts and prospective converts to the Faith in other regions of the globe. The simplest answer to that question is the fact that the Jesuit colleges and universities in the United States have come in the last twenty years to open their doors—first in the graduate departments, later in all departments—to Negroes, not to speak of Orientals and other races or peoples frequently discriminated against in our country. Today more than twelve hundred Negroes are studying in American Jesuit high schools, colleges, and universities. (Exact figures are difficult to obtain, since not all schools make a practice of registering the racial origin of their applicants.) More important than these bald figures, however, is the spirit underlying such integration: a spirit of truly Christian world fraternity that has developed in the entire American Catholic educational sphere in the last fifteen or twenty years.

In the promotion of such an interracial spirit, Jesuit educators have taken an active part, encouraged by their own world headquarters in Rome, by the forward-looking action of so many members of the American Hierarchy, and by the Popes themselves. Such men as the two brothers, Father William M. and Father John P. Markoe (the latter a West Point graduate and classmate of President Eisenhower); Father George H. Dunne, of Phoenix, Arizona; Father Claude H. Heithaus, of Milwaukee; Father John E. Coogan, of Detroit; the Southern sociologists and authors, Fathers Joseph H. Fichter, Louis J. Twomey, Raymond Bernard, and Albert S. Foley, are among many who in recent years have made their voices heard in protest against racial injustice. Superiors of the different provinces, especially in the Southern Province (New

Orleans), parish priests, editors and writers, professors, school administrators, retreat and Sodality directors and missionaries at home and abroad have worked in recent years to put the Society on record for thoroughgoing interracial justice. Most Jesuit schools and Jesuit-directed student or lay organizations feature today some planned activity in this regard. In New York, the Catholic Interracial Council, under the author's direction, helps to service with inspiration and information twenty-six other Catholic Interracial Councils around the country. The Society's own novitiates do not make a distribution of race or color in considering the qualifications of candidates.

The world mission work of Christ's Church has, in recent years, come into agonizing conflict with world Communism's organized attack on Christianity. American Jesuits are exiled from China or imprisoned in that unhappy country, while exiled Jesuit brethren of Communist-dominated Eastern Europe are guests in our American institutions. Father Edmund A. Walsh, S.J., of Georgetown University, who personally visited Soviet Russia as director of the papal famine relief expedition to that country in 1921, did yeoman's work with his addresses and writings to alert the American conscience as to the virulence of the Communist plague; and the American Jesuit weekly, *America*, published in New York City, specialized in analyzing the situation the Soviet revolution had created, in Russia and in the world.

In accordance with the policies inaugurated by the late Father General Ledóchowski—policies carried on by his present successor, Father Janssens—American Jesuits in treating this question (whether by word or action) have kept consistently clear two complementary ideas, neither of which is workable without the other. First, that Communism cannot be combated by fear, nor any battle won by fighting in the dark. For this reason the public needs a steady flow of accurate knowledge: knowledge of the actual situation in Russia and Communist-controlled countries, and of world Communism's innumerable activities and infiltrations. Second, that a merely negative program is doomed to frustration; it is necessary to bring the whole weight of Christian social teaching and method to bear upon the grave social, racial, and economic abuses that are Communism's hunting or breeding ground. This latter requirement, much the more difficult of the two, means that we get nowhere without a thorough study of the Christian social order, both in theory and practice. Mere playing by ear can result in as much harm as good. For this reason, American Jesuits some years ago decided to take the bull by the horns, and organized among their own personnel an Institute of Social Order, with headquarters at the University of St. Louis. In recent years the Institute, for which some of the Society's best men are set aside, concentrates especially on the analysis of social questions, such as the family and marriage, wage and trade union problems, women's work, and so on; and young Jesuits are encouraged to take an interest in such questions and their application to the acute problems of the day.

The missionary priest is frequently obliged to take a hand personally in starting or administering social and charitable projects which at home would be cared for by the regular organized agencies. Dealing directly with people in dire destitution, he has to show initiative and resourcefulness if his mission work is not to perish from the weight of sheer misery. This enables him in turn to counsel others in similar needs. So with American Jesuit missions, as some of our photographs depict. Father Marion M. Ganey, of the Honduras mission, was asked by the Governor of Fiji to start co-operatives in those islands, and is now embarked on a two-year program in New Zealand organizing co-ops. In the Philippines, a new combined board for social work has been established under the expert leadership of Father Walter B. Hogan, S.J., industrial relations apostle of the Islands. The vigorous form and enthusiastic language of Father John P. Sullivan, apostle of the West Indian co-operative movement, are known all through the Caribbean region. Alaska's changing economy poses difficult problems for the Eskimos, who are obliged to work in the canning factories during the traditional hunting season. To help organize the men and protect their rights, Father G. S. Endal became a member of the union, organized his men into the CIO and stood by them in a strike. Father Paul C. O'Connor, veteran Alaska Jesuit missionary, is active in the Federal Housing Administration. Alaska has now a Jesuit college and high school at Copper Centre, where Eskimo boys can obtain that dearest of all prizes—each a private room of his own.

American Jesuits conduct five seminaries for native clergy, two of them major seminaries. They conduct also twelve colleges in the mission territory, of which two are universities (the Ateneo of Manila and the Ateneo of Cagayan, in the Philippines).

Today, with the disappearance of the colonial regimes, the missionary is expected to contribute something tangible and definite to the welfare of the country where he operates. Hence the essential importance of educational and social welfare work in the missions. Fruitful contribution, however, involves the much more difficult problem of adaptation: the vast and intricate question as to how the Christian message should be conveyed to people whose culture and traditions differ so profoundly from our own. These and many kindred questions are discussed by the representatives of all the Catholic leading mission-sending organizations of the United States who meet each summer for Fordham University's Mission Institute, under the general guidance of the anthropologist and ethnologist, Father J. Franklin Ewing, S.J.

Fathers John T. Newell, John C. Murphy, and
Charles I. Prendergast watching the children of

Minas-Deroro, British Honduras, rehearsing for
their fiesta in the square of this ancient village.

Rev. Robert L. Hodapp, S. J. in a classroom of Holy
Redeemer School at Belize, British Honduras.

Rev. John M. Knopp, S. J., Father Superior of the Honduras mission, in front of the new St. John's College at Belize, which replaced building destroyed in hurricane.

Most Rev. David F. Hickey, S.J. watches the girls of Holy Redeemer School decorate the picture of Our Lady of Guadalupe.

The people of Belize in an evening candlelight procession in honor of Our Lady of Guadalupe, Protectress against the dreadful hurricane.

Left: Rev. Marion M. Ganey, S. J. talking to the fishermen members of a cooperative he founded at San Pedro Cay.

The old Spanish cathedral in the village of Minas-Deroro.

Left: Blessing the children at Minas de San Antone.

Father Newell blessing water and seed corn. The
vessel in foreground is an ancient baptismal font.

Rev. William Ulrich, S. J. and Mayan Indians of British Honduras.

Father Ganey sailing to San Pedro Cay.

CONCLUSION

IN these few pages I have been interested only in showing that the Jesuits are here, as an active contributing element in the American community. This, after all, needs no great demonstration, simply an acquaintance with what is going on in the educational and religious world.

It would have been useful, and doubtless interesting, to have devoted more time to the curiously prolific crop of legends that grew up around the Jesuits, mostly in the seventeenth and eighteenth centuries. Some of these have even passed into our language, so that people use the term "jesuitical" as synony-

mous with crafty, subtle, or underhanded. Just a simple instance, one out of thousands. I happened the other day to look
into Neil McAlpine's *Gaelic Dictionary* (Edinburgh, 1903).
It is a competent, intelligent work, but it defines "Jesuit" as
feall-creideach (*feall*, deceitful; *creideach*, believer), a deceitful believer: such, and nothing more. That is all that this
learned Highlander knew of our Society. Yet he is properly
indignant at Dr. Samuel Johnson for calumniating the Gaels.

Hardiest of all these legends is the notion that the Jesuits
teach, or did teach at one time, the doctrine that the end justi-
fies the means. According to such teaching, it would be com-
mendable to bump off your neighbor if thereby you erase a
troublesome heretic, and so on. The historical origin of such
legends and the proofs of their falsity have already been
treated by many wholly competent authorities. As for the
"end-justifies-the-means" doctrine, a prize of one thousand
marks was offered in Germany in 1852, subject to a wholly
impartial jury (the law faculties of either Heidelberg or
Bonn), to anybody who could demonstrate that Jesuits ever
had or did teach such a notion, but the demonstration never
was produced.* The most obvious comment upon any and all
such legends is that no self-respecting person today would join
the Jesuits, or remain at night under any Jesuit roof, if he
believed such stories were true. On the contrary, the Jesuit
shares the heavy moral responsibility of the Church herself,

* "It has never been proved, and never can be proved (although the attempt has frequently been made), that the Jesuits ever taught the nefarious
proposition ascribed to them, which would be entirely subversive of all
morality." These are the words of an Anglican writer, Rev. Richard Littledale
(*Encyclopedia Britannica*, 11th ed.).

which like Thomas à Becket, martyred Archbishop of Canter-
bury, cannot yield even to the most appealing human sentiment where questions of ultimate right or wrong are concerned. How many convenient "ends" could be achieved, how
many agonizing impasses avoided, if Catholic teaching could
agree to permit artificial contraception, or the remarriage of
divorced persons, or the legitimacy of certain highly profitable
but morally dubious business practices! The Jesuit, preaching
the Church's doctrine, has no desire to make the course of
right conduct any harder or narrower than Christ our Lord
meant it to be, and sometimes he may be criticized by the
more severe-minded for his conscientiousness in this respect.
But there can be no yielding where right principles are in-
volved.

On the other hand, it is quite normal, in the course of
human affairs, that the Society, following in the footsteps of
the Master after whom it is named, may disturb certain
anxious minds by its readiness to go to the limit, as it were, in
furthering the Master's cause. It will always create a certain
scandal by its opposition to nationalism, racialism, and other
unnatural divisions of humanity, by its stress upon the more
universal good as something to be preferred over the more particular, however worthy that may be. The spirit of the Society,
as its great saints and leaders have continually reminded it, is
a certain holy recklessness, a readiness for the seed to be buried
in the ground in order that it may bear fruit, a spirit driving
forward always to greater and greater works for God's glory.

Such a spirit can easily be misunderstood, especially if people think that God's glory means something we can somehow

add of ourselves to His perfection. We cannot place God in our debt, but God gives to us: forever communicates Himself to us. To work His glory is to make ourselves and others more and more capable of receiving His gifts, and thus being more truly men, more truly human and—by sharing in His life—divine. And that is a goal we can pursue without setting bounds to our own effort or ingenuity. The fact that interested or shortsighted people in the history of the Church have occasionally confused God's glory with their own personal ambition does not impair the holiness and purity of the goal.

The Jesuits disturb some people, too, because in all this outventuring for God's honor they insist upon acting not as individuals but as members of a cohesive and highly organized group, a Society or Company, not an aggregation of starry-eyed idealists. None acts for himself alone, but always as the member of a co-operative body where the members own all things in common: pray, suffer, rejoice, live, and merit as one. And this united body itself considers itself of no significance except as part of the universal Church, Christ's world-wide Mystical Body.

Seen in the concrete, this unity or cohesion means discipline, it spells obedience, it requires rules and regulations, it implies much that is uncomfortable for human pride and easygoing ways. People sometimes praise the Jesuits for their discipline, as if in a literal sense they were some kind of military order, as if discipline and efficiency were the Society's major aim. But if discipline and efficiency were the be-all and end-all of the Society, I doubt if many people, especially in modern America, would be eager to join or particularly willing to stay.

If we yearn for army life, we can find plenty of it elsewhere. The hundreds of World War II veterans who have joined the Jesuits and other religious communities in the last ten years are not particularly keen on signing up for a lifelong regimentation. Men are drawn immediately, permanently, deeply, not by glamor or marching ranks or corporate display, but by one motive and one motive alone, which is love. As the Founder of the Jesuits says in the prologue of his Constitutions, the law by which his members bind themselves is the law of love: love for God, love for the God-man Jesus Christ, love for all men because God loves them and made them.

The Jesuit order claims to be a valid way, a path to the leading of a perfect Christian life, but it is still up to each individual as to the faithfulness by which he follows that path.

Jesuits, being human beings, can be tempted to be boastful, and members of any prominent organization can, and sometimes do, become overfascinated with its particular perfections. The Society expanded so miraculously during its first century, so many of its members achieved marvels of holiness and learning, and it was subjected to so much unreasoning criticism, that it would have been a miracle if individual Jesuits had not appeared who had yielded to the temptation of pious self-gratulation. But these remained individuals, and the sin of corporate pride cannot be justly ascribed to the Society. Ignatius in his Constitutions had warned against just this sort of thing, telling his members they should be particularly careful to avoid comparisons with other organizations in the Church. Jesuits, to their honor be it said, have been observant on this point ever since. They talk about their own affairs among themselves, but their talk (with only very rare exceptions) is blessedly free from aspersions against or comparisons with other religious Orders or states of ecclesiastical life.

With this in mind, we can better estimate the significance of pictures such as are found in a book like this. A picture book does not itself tell a story: it appeals to the imagination. The photographs capture some of the imaginative appeal of the Jesuit Order. I only regret that the bare bones of factual information prevented me from projecting more of this imaginative appeal onto the book's limited screen.

Ignatius loved and honored the imagination; he treated it as a very precious gift of God, and insisted that people who experienced the *Spiritual Exercises* should deliberately arouse their imaginations so as to help them anchor spiritual ideas and attitudes in their minds. Following the example of many of the older spiritual guides of the Church, such as St. Bernard of Clairvaux, he explained in homely detail how we could reconstruct the life of Jesus by intelligent use of the imagination, and he clothed in unforgettable imaginative forms his great proposals for making life decisions.

The early Jesuits in their educational system laid great stress upon the cultivation of the poetic and rhetorical imagination. The Order took its great upward swing during the Baroque period, when poets, playwrights, painters, sculptors, and architects vied with one another in the creation of florid, highly dramatic images, combined usually with an astonishing degree of technical skill. Ecstatic saints' poses, floating angels, glimpses of heaven through openings in the midst of an archway, as in southern Bavaria's incredible *Wieskirche,* rich gilded carvings and skilful lavishing of space and proportion; cheerful, buoyant, sentimental pageants of movement and light; in a more subdued field, curiously engraved emblems and frontispieces, delicate bindings on precious books, graceful furniture, flamboyant altar furnishings and church vestments; all helped to elevate the mind to the Heavenly Court at a time when courts were stately and culture was lavish in satin, tooled leather and rich brocades.

The Baroque imagination was not Ignatius' imagination, for he lived before that time and thought and spoke in simpler and more austere terms. But through the commentators, the teachers, and the builders of Jesuit churches the style became identified with the Jesuits: so that people today speak of Baroque architecture as "Jesuit architecture" as if the Jesuits had somehow invented it. True, the Jesuits adopted this architecture in a great number of their churches; they liked it because it was the style of the period, also because the Baroque churches were spacious, fitted for preaching, and enabled the people to see and follow the services at the altar. Practical-minded men, the Jesuits favored what—in contrast to the medieval churches—was a highly practical style. But the Society was not wedded then to any one style of architecture, nor is it so today. The famous Gesù Church in Rome, the first great Jesuit Church, was not planned by the Jesuits, although Jesuit churches around the world have been built in imitation of the original Gesù.

Jesuits today feel tenderly toward the Baroque and will never let it be forgotten, for the age and the style are both associated with much that is precious in their history. But the Society is not committed to any one artistic or imaginative idiom. A Jesuit church can be built in the wholly contemporary, functional style of the mid-twentieth century quite as appropriately as if it were modelel upon the Gesù in Rome, provided it complies in all other respects with what the Catholic Church expects of an edifice devoted to her liturgical worship and pastoral needs.

One of the most acute problems of the Church in the modern world is the right philosophy of the imagination. If imagination usurps the place of reason, the effect is intellectual and spiritual chaos; for reason, under God and with the help of God's grace, is man's guide. Hence the cultivation of man's rational powers. With all Ignatius' use of the imagination, he always leads a man to the point where he must reason, and reason closely, about the affairs of his own and his neighbor's life.

Yet reason cannot function without imagination, without the use of symbols, metaphors, and analogies, and a certain warmth of feeling toward the truth itself. The immense changes in present human living, the incessant appeals to human emotion by a continued onslaught of vivid visual and aural images, confuse the bearing of time-honored symbols, and words themselves lose their sap and meaning.

It may, therefore, not be too great a hazard to suggest that the Society, which did so much to elevate and enrich the imaginative content of European culture in the seventeenth and eighteenth centuries, may have some such mission today. Art, sacred and profane, with its laws and deeper significance, has had rather short shrift in American Jesuit schools, with a few happy exceptions. Yet by that neglect may we not be losing one of the main keys to the modern mind? Jesuit educators are already becoming concerned over this problem.

In every Jesuit's life there comes a time when the Lord begins to knock on his door and suggest to him that his life-work is coming to an end. Sometimes the tap is gentle and in-sinuating, sometimes it is blunt and imperious; but the Gospel has warned us too often in the daily Mass for anyone to be indifferent to death's approach. Father Daniel A. Lord, the most widely-known and widely-loved American Jesuit in our time, received not long before his death in 1955 the very plain notice, through his physician, that with cancer of the lungs his life-remainder might be short, or it might be some years, but go he must. (Ironically enough, Father Lord, an exuber-antly jovial person, neither smoked nor used any alcoholic drink.)

This presented a problem to Father Lord, as it does to any Jesuit when such a moment comes. With so much that he had hoped still to do for God and man, how employ the short time that is left? To die of cancer, Father Lord told his friends, was a privilege; he had no quarrel with that part of the arrange-ment. But with daily weakening strength, how crowd so much into so little? He managed, however, to direct from his sickbed an immense public pageant he had planned at Toronto, and found time to write a book, *The Man Who Was Really Santa Claus,* publish several articles and pamphlets, and finish his autobiography before the end came.

The late Father Daniel Lord in closeup, and accompanying the singing of some young members of the Sodality of Our Lady.

Father Lord was much in the public eye, as he himself explained, because of the spectacular field in which he operated. Officially he was most widely identified for many years as the National Director of the Sodality of the Blessed Virgin, an action-organization for young and old which dates back to the earliest years of the Society. Practically, since we are looking at pictures of American Jesuits, the wonder of Daniel Lord's life was the operative imagination that he crowded into all his work for the young—and for the old folk as well. He himself summed up his work under three main headings:

To make religion live in all the departments of life, teaching great audiences of young and old, in one big city after another in the United States, how to get *started* on making their religion live. His aim was a working system, by which religion and life are one.

To open to the American public a vast perspective of religion's joyfulness—the joy and honor of professing it openly, frankly, taking it out of the sacristy straight into the theater or the ballroom. He believed, he said, in recreational opportunities that are "creative, exhaustive, and fairly exhausting." He had his young people—sometimes three thousand of them at a time—begin a religious program by singing the latest popular disc hit; and he had them end a dance with night prayers. His innumerable songfests, with himself at the piano, were "icebreakers" for more serious fare to follow.

His prolific popular writings, mostly in pamphlet form, supplied for his public what he greatly valued: "plain, honest answers to the questions of today."

The "spectacular" Father Lord is, by his happy memory, a part of the American Jesuit scene. So, too, is the patient analyzer of moral problems, Father Gerald Kelly, of St. Mary's, Kansas; or the subtle philosopher and theologian, Father John Courtney Murray, of Woodstock, who is particularly keen on finding the true bearings of religious liberty upon the conscience of Catholics and non-Catholics alike in our America of many creeds. So likewise are the Jesuits highly active in public, civic life—educational administrators or parish priests—who are helping to present to the American people a true picture of what the Church means for our country's welfare in every sense of the word. Jesuits consider it as a genuine part of the great general campaign for right and justice when people hear, as they frequently do, about such notables as Fordham's eloquent ex-president, Father Robert I. Gannon, now rector of St. Ignatius Loyola parish and residence in New York City; or St. Louis University's president, Father Paul Reinert; or San Francisco's Father William J. Dunne, or others too numerous to mention. Yet Jesuits know, too, that the men who loom large in the public eye are neither more nor less than the army of others of whom less, or little, or practically nothing is heard.

It is the joint work of the Society that counts, for they are one fraternity united through the world in a common effort; yet it is not the Society's work, but that of the whole Church that counts: Jesus Christ in all His members realizing His full stature. This universal work will go on, Jesuits or no Jesuits, until the end of time. American Jesuits are grateful that they have now some part or parcel in the whole undertaking. If this story of what they have achieved or are still achieving may inspire others to rival and to far exceed them, their deepest wish will be fulfilled.

PART THREE

NOTE

NOTE BY
MARGARET BOURKE-WHITE

WHEN *Life* assigned me to do a photographic essay on the American Jesuits all I knew about the Society of Jesus was that it existed. "It will be like exploring a whole new country," I told my editors, and I accepted the assignment eagerly. I had underestimated my subject. It was like exploring a whole new world.

I found this world populated by some energetic and extraordinary personalities who had permeated most of the activities that are important to mankind: labor-management relations, education of countless kinds, medicine, astronomy, geology, seismology, aviation, exploration, radio, Hollywood, the problem of race relations, the simultaneous-translation system used by the United Nations, the soundless world of the deaf, missions the world over.

To cover this enormous subject we tried to plan at *Life* a sampling that would give a representative Jesuit cross section. With Claude Stanush, then *Life's* Religion editor, and Michael Arlen, Jr. (who worked with me on the Jesuit essay until he was interrupted in mid-stream by being drafted), we drew up an itinerary that included key points all over the United States: St. Louis, New Orleans, Los Angeles, Santa Clara, San Francisco, Georgetown, Maryland, Poughkeepsie, New York, and many points in between. We were emphasizing the *American* Jesuits, and the pictures were all to be taken in the United States with the important exception of foreign missions in Honduras, which the Jesuits place under their St. Louis Province.

During my six months on the story I found the Jesuits always full of surprises. I never knew what to expect, but I knew that in each place I visited I would find a devout and dedicated man—and probably a witty one. And I never would have guessed I could have so much sheer fun photographing a company of priests. Underneath their jokes and witticisms was a quiet happiness of deep dedication which I sensed vividly and respected greatly.

Some Fathers were experts in their respective fields, as for example Father Daniel Linehan, director of the Weston Observatory and famous seismologist. Father Linehan was the first of the Fathers with whom I worked to any great extent, and he was quite unlike my preconceived idea of a priest. I was to meet him at my hotel in Boston, but when I stepped out of the elevator I could not find anybody in the lobby who even looked like a priest. There was not a cassock in sight. When a genial, hearty-looking man in what was probably the brightest red plaid shirt on the New England seaboard came up and introduced himself at Father Linehan, I could hardly conceal my surprise. (Later I learned that those Fathers who do exceptionally rough outdoor work may wear mufti in the field, but permission must be given.)

The project on which he allowed me to accompany him was to test out a site in the Kennebec River for the building of a power dam. We drove to Maine in a station wagon and stayed at a tiny tourist camp in a little town called "The Forks," close to the Canadian border. Every day we broke our way on foot through miles of thick forest to the river. The men carried the equipment on their backs to the Kennebec where the Father strode through the rapids, set off his dynamite charges, and analyzed the results.

Every morning in the early dawn Father Linehan said Mass, either in his little cabin with the linoleum floor, or in the open forest. He had a portable Mass kit which had traveled halfway around the globe and bore labels like a much-traveled suitcase. For services in the woods the Father supported the altar on empty dynamite cases, always in plentiful supply since he used dynamite in his work. His talented young helper, Father James Skehan, gathered longleafed ferns and decorated the altar support beautifully.

A day of work in the Kennebec River was also a day of

Father Daniel Linehan leading a field crew through the Maine woods, to the Kennebec River to investigate by seismic methods the choice of a new dam site. In photograph at right he is interpreting the seismograms.

laughter. Father Linehan had a talent for tucking an unexpected play on words—even when these were technical or geological words—into almost every sentence. But one evening when we were homeward bound after a particularly satisfying discovery about the rock character of the river, I saw a different side to his character.

"Take today," he said. "Today when I read my seismograph there were only two who knew that rock was down there under sixty feet of water. Only God and I knew. And to think this is the same God who came down to our altar this morning, the same God who made that rock, who made all the rocks in the world.

"I would give up all my seismology to celebrate one such Mass as you came to this morning. Think of all the energy stored up in the world—all that power. That is God. And I held Him in my hand this morning. That's why I am happy. That's why I'm a priest."

Shortly after I worked with him, Father Linehan journeyed to the North Magnetic Pole, then sailed with the "Atka" to the region of the South Pole. I like to think that far under the massive ice caps of both our earthly poles are rocky secrets known only to Father Linehan and God.

The extraordinary devotion of Father Linehan to his seismic profession was matched by other Jesuit Fathers in other humbler fields—even in the field of raising hogs. I made this —to me—exciting discovery in British Honduras while visiting the Jesuit mission at the tiny hill-post of San Antonio. The hog episode caught my imagination particularly because on earlier trips through India and South Africa I had fre-

Father William Ulrich supervising hog-weighing at San Antonio.

quently been struck with the hardships that result when people of a primitive culture are flung into the twentieth century without a knowledge of the values of the twentieth century to guide them. Here in the lonely Honduran hills, a tribe of Mayan Indians—their faces like fine carvings of polished wood—furnished a classic case. Like agricultural people the world over, the Mayans counted their wealth in livestock—mainly hogs. They were at the mercy of the buyer who bought the hogs on sight at an arbitrary price. A fat hog, a lean hog, the villagers could not measure the difference.

About five years before my visit, Father William Ulrich, an earnest soft-spoken man who had studied some of these problems while preparing for the priesthood in St. Louis University, brought to the village something new: a pair of scales. The gift of the scales revolutionized the economic life of the village. Pigs were sold by the pound. The next step was to put more pounds on the pig. Father introduced scientific agriculture, taught the people to rotate crops, taught them how to improve the fodder. As the hogs grew finer and heavier, the price per pound quadrupled. The rising spiral that commenced with the scales transformed San Antonio into a prosperous village.

Father Ulrich's triumph with the pig is in the direct tradition of the Order. Through the centuries, beginning with the great traveler St. Francis Xavier, Jesuit Fathers have followed the policy of moving into a practical situation, becoming immersed in its problems, and winning a following from kings to peasants by coming up with workable answers.

Strong in this tradition is Father Marion M. Ganey, from

Gillespie, Illinois, whom I met in the large central Jesuit Mission in Belize. Father Ganey, tall, dark, and with a Lincoln-esque profile, has pioneered in establishing credit unions and co-operatives among the people of British Honduras. One of these is a "fishermen's credit union" through which the men build up a fund from which to draw without interest in time of need, as when the dreaded hurricane damages the fishing boats. Another is a "chicle co-operative" whose members draw sap from the trees for chewing gum. During my visit, Father Ganey was busy negotiating a contract on behalf of the "chicleros" with one of the biggest chewing-gum manufacturers in America.

Equally in the tradition of the Order—for throughout their history Jesuits have staged plays and pageants—Father Ganey put on a cycle of the Coventry Plays at Panta Gorda, a small Honduran mission where he had previously been stationed. The people took to the Elizabethan English beautifully, he told me. The only difficulty was in getting anyone to play the bad angels.

After the success of the plays he taught the people to put on public debates, discussing such close-to-home subjects as: Which is better—a thatched roof or a tin roof? "I wanted them to learn to speak up," Father Ganey told me, pointing out that the debates, like the credit unions, were part of his campaign to train the people to help themselves. "It's a good missionary," he explained, "who can work himself out of a job." This he seems to have done. Recently I received a letter from Suva Fiji, to which he has been transferred and where he is now setting up credit unions for the Fiji Islanders.

Father Gregory Sontag uses sound amplifier to announce his arrival at Sittee River mission, and is greeted by parishioners.

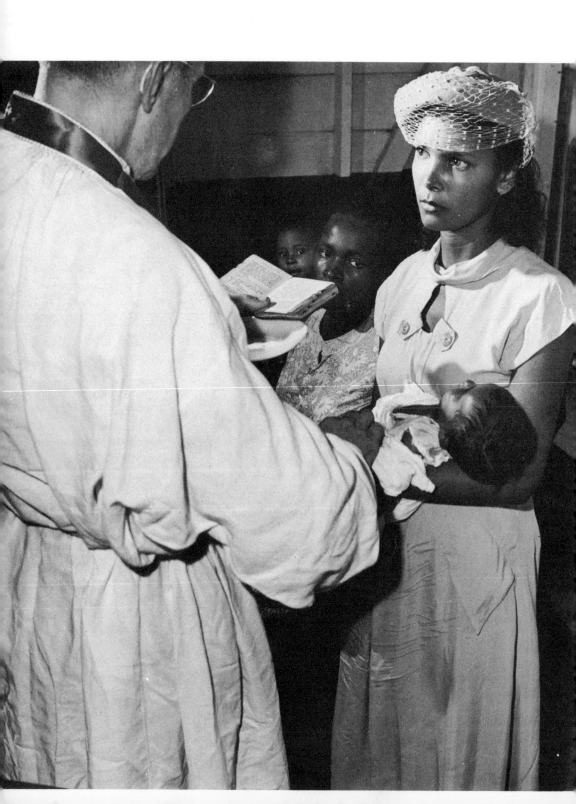

The sacraments of Baptism and Penance are administered by Father Sontag.

A rather different personality from the other Jesuit missionaries with whom I worked in Honduras is Father Gregory Sontag from Mankato, Michigan. Father Sontag has the pale blazing eyes of the crusader, the weather-beaten skin of the sailor, and a reputation as a gifted mechanic. Indeed he needs to be. His work takes him to settlements hidden deep away in the swampy jungles where no means of communication exists except the trackless waterways. Working out of Stan Creek on the Honduran Gulf, Father Sontag travels his mission rounds in an arc-shaped boat named the *Teresita* after the patron of travelers, and fitted with a capricious engine that only the Father can tame.

On his mission rounds, Father Sontag uses his mechanical talents in various ways, as Michael Arlen and I discovered when we accompanied him to a remote river post. Once we had crossed a choppy arm of Honduras Gulf and turned into the quiet waters of the Sittee River, Father Sontag set up a portable electronic microphone on the roof of the *Teresita*. Although we could see only water and jungle without a human being in sight, the Father plunged confidently into his program. First he played a couple of records from the large supply he carried, and when the strains of "Ain't She Sweet" had died away over the steaming swamplands, he began his announcements "Rosary meeting in Middle Bank tonight. Magic lantern slides. Come everybody. No charge; no charge. Early Mass tomorrow morning, come everybody, no charge."

As though a magic wand had touched the river, its deserted waters came alive with little boats. These were cigar-shaped craft carved out of a single giant tree trunk and precariously

packed with the Father's parishioners. Arriving at the tiny
Middle Bank Church, Father Sontag accepted a bouquet of
wild red hibiscus which he placed on the altar; then he hooked
up his magic lantern and with his congregation sitting in awe-
struck silence he ran off his brightly colored religious slides,
and conducted his Rosary service.

After Rosary the boats disappeared into the night. Father
Sontag read his Office by lamplight, crawled under his mos-
quito net to snatch a little sleep, and at dawn was ready at the
riverside to welcome the small fleet of dugouts bringing wor-
shipers to Mass.

In the mountainous heart of the Spanish-speaking Republic
of Honduras, Michael Arlen and I visited Jesuit missions
which could be reached only by mule. We had chartered a
plane which landed on a grassy plateau in the hills. A convoy
of mules met our plane. My cameras, tripod, and cases of film
and flashbulbs were strapped to the animal's backs, Mike and
I were assisted into the unfamiliar saddles, and we rode seven
miles through the forest to Minas de Oro.

This lovely old Spanish town was to be a headquarters for
us during our work in the mountains. The splendid mission
here had been the single-handed work of Father John T.
Newell of Denver, Colorado. His latest addition was an ex-
cellent little library. Traveling with us were Father George P.
Prendergast and Father John C. Murphy of St. Louis. Father
Murphy, who had been kindly loaned to us by the Father
Superior, looked surprisingly like actor John Wayne.

With the three priests Michael Arlen and I traveled on the
mission rounds. Frequently we had to break through solid

jungle where the mountain trails had become completely overgrown since the Fathers' last visit. Frequently we had to ride back after dark through tropical rains, lighting our mules' way as they bore us down the steep, slippery rocks, with hand-held flashlights.

Most vividly I remember the joy of the children when these kindly Fathers appeared on a visit. Just in sight of Minas de San Antonio a child spotted us, ran down the hill to Father Murphy as fast as his little legs could carry him. He wanted to be the first child to be blessed. The church of San Antonio was ruined in the 1952 hurricane, but protected in one partially intact corner was an ancient, exquisite Spanish confession rail and a large round two-hundred-year-old font. While Father Prendergast listened to confessions Father Newell stood beside the lovely font and blessed the water that the women brought in gourds and saucepans, then blessed the seed corn with which they would plant next year's crop.

Back in the United States, I began working along the wharves of Philadelphia and Wilmington with Father Dennis Comey, famous waterfront priest. Father Comey, specialist in labor-management relations, is as much at home on a coal barge or dock as one of the longshoremen with whom he works. Gray-haired, keen of eye, Father Comey founded his St. Joseph's College of Industrial Relations in Philadelphia in 1943. In 1951 he became an arbitrator on the stormy Philadelphia waterfront. His heart is in his school. "I accept the role of arbitrator," he says, "because then I can prove that my teachings are soundly practical." Both stevedores and shippers have great confidence in Father Comey.

The thing that impressed me immediately about Father Comey was his quiet insistence on getting firsthand information. On the Philadelphia waterfront, we boarded a large sugar barge where he had been called to judge whether the cargo was "distressed" (shifting and dangerous). If so, the men who unloaded it would be entitled to extra pay. In a matter of minutes the Father had scampered down a ladder into the deep, dim hold. Suddenly he began kicking the sugar bags. I knew that with the well-tempered Father Comey, this could not be in anger. "What is he doing?" I asked one of the stevedores. I was told he was judging the moisture content, deciding whether the bags were damp when they were on-loaded, which would make the cargo heavier and more treacherous.

A small thing perhaps, but to me it was eloquent. I found it impressive that a priest could kick a bag of sugar and get so much meaning from it.

My long journey among the Jesuits ended at Phoenix, Arizona, where I went to see something of the work of the Society of Jesus in combating race prejudice.

A brilliant Jesuit, Father George H. Dunne, had been posted in Phoenix since 1948 and had done effective work against color prejudice in this notoriously difficult spot. Father Dunne began working quietly and thoughtfully with Director Alton Thomas of the National Urban League. These two men, and others, tried to get the law which required segregation repealed. The people had voted against desegregation, and the most the Father and his group could do was to get the law changed enough so that each school district was autonomous on the integration question. Thus it was of the highest importance to win over the Boards of Education and public opinion as well.

At this point, Father Dunne came out boldly as a priest and called segregation a sin. This had a tremendous influence on Catholics. It was one thing to have prejudice and another to understand it as a sin against Christ.

My own arrival in Phoenix coincided happily with the opening of Phoenix Union High School to Negroes. Father Dunne and Mr. Thomas took me proudly through the school. In the Human Relations class, Negro and white children were having a lively and unself-conscious discussion group. Out on the recreation grounds, Negro and white girls were playing volleyball together.

One of the leaders in pointing out that Christians had no choice on the question of prejudice against human beings because of race or color was the editor for many years of *America,* and is still an associate editor of the review: Father John LaFarge, with whom I have had the pleasure of collaborating on this book.

Father LaFarge became interested in the problem of racial injustice as a young priest in Maryland. His work toward integration is a theme that has guided his whole life. When the Supreme Court laid down its historic desegregation mandate in 1954, Father LaFarge said this was in a way the fulfillment of his life's mission. November of 1955 brought him to his Golden Anniversary: fifty years as a Jesuit and as a priest. For his thoughtful and knowledgeable collaboration on this book, I am profoundly grateful.

There are many Jesuit Fathers who gave me generous help

Rev. John LaFarge, S. J.

and valued friendship as I gathered my material, and who deserve greater recognition than this book has space to give them. I have only tried to sketch a few. I thank all who helped make possible the pictures for *Life* and this book—all among this varied company of multi-talented Fathers who opened doors of understanding as I traveled on my photographic mission.

This work began with Father Linehan, the seismologist, the unlocker of the earth's secrets, the practicing scientist. It ended on the doorstep of Father LaFarge, the philosopher, the humanitarian, the practicing man of letters. And thus—in a way—these two stand at opposite ends of the Jesuit spectrum, held together in common bonds of piety and dedication.

Novices gathering in grapes from the vineyard of
the Sacred Heart Novitiate, at Los Gatos, California.